PAINFUL MIRACLES

When Walking Through Pain Puts Us on the Path of Miraculous Breakthrough

Principles and Lessons Learned on the Front Lines of Fighting Human Trafficking

BENNY YU

Edited by Audrey Sileci and Janet Jun
Cover Design by Dalia Vázquez

Author's website: www.painfulmiracles.com

Benny Yu
910 W 17th Street
Suite B
Santa Ana, CA 92706

To all who fight for freedom and justice

Table of Contents

Foreword
by Dave Gibbons

Fun.

Crazy.

Wild.

Passionate.

Gentle.

Loving.

Heart.

Leader of leaders.

Basketball.

This is Benny Yu to me.

I've known Benny since the days he went to seminary. I've seen him grow as a husband, father, and now a leader of leaders globally.

He's been recognized for his work by organizations in America, Mexico, Brazil, and several European countries, as well as the United Nations. But this is only of late. I've seen Benny doing necessary work before people even noticed he exists. He was doing the work before the work.

Much of that labor is in the crucible of life, where all the support you had that makes you feel significant is burned away. Your titles, academic credentials, successes, and achievements are gone. You're left with nothing but you. It becomes about who you are without all the props. It's who you are, whether you are praised or criticized.

Benny has been through so much. As a child, he faced horrific attacks on who he is. Yet Benny has eyes to see even his past like God does. He went to Thailand with me and a group of young leaders to "change the world." While we did some good, the real changes probably happened within us. In Thailand, Benny received the downloads he needed about himself and his future to embark on an adventure to Mexico and beyond.

I've seen Benny play in intense basketball games on pavement. I've witnessed him launch his work in Mexico with no promise of financing, and I visited him after he almost got killed. We've cried together.

We've also had some of the best belly laughs in the world together walking through the colorful streets of Mexico City, Bangkok, L.A., and São Paulo. Of course, as we walked, we made sure to eat all the street food we saw along the way. To this day, I owe Benny for taking me to the best "taco al pastor" stand in the world near Coyoacán. Yes, the best in the world.

Benny's life is a miracle. So is his journey experiencing God's provision. I love this guy. You will too, as you see his heart unveiled in this book.

I'm so glad Benny wrote this book. *Painful Miracles* is really his life, how God can turn brokenness into beauty. Benny is a modern-day Jesus follower who truly believes that Narnia is real. May you see the world and yourself as he does. If you do, you'll taste Heaven every day.

Introduction

Many people consider the word "painful" an inaccurate description of a miracle. Miracles are supposed to free us from pain, so the two words are not typically connected. Please don't get me wrong; I am fully confident that miracles deliver us from suffering. However, this book proposes that most of the time, there is a process of addressing our pain that leads us on a path to a miracle. Unfortunately, because many of us fear or avoid pain, we often miss out on the miraculous.

I would like to share with you my stories of walking through suffering and hopelessness to find miracles on the other end. These personal experiences, as well as those from over a decade fighting human trafficking on the front lines, taught me some important Kingdom principles, which I'm certain can help you in your own process of healing, restoration, and expectation of the miraculous.

The journey that we are about to take together is going to challenge how you address your past hurts, your present-day battles, and your tomorrow. It may also trigger some unwanted memories, but don't lose heart. Remember that God promised His constant presence and His Holy Spirit as a helper and counselor in times of trouble. I wish I could offer all the answers for your healing in this book, but that's not my job; it's the Holy Spirit's job. What I can do is share about the parts of our healing that we are responsible for, help you understand how to surrender the rest, and address the steps of faith we all need to take into the unknown. My hope is that as I share, your faith will increase to the point of believing that the miraculous will come out of discomfort, brokenness, and uncertainty. We've got to first break through blockades in our minds before we can experience a breakthrough in our lives. Even more importantly, every breakthrough we experience comes with greater responsibility.

At the end of every chapter, I included a section that will walk you through a process of moving beyond reflection into a personal experience with each principle. This may slow down your reading, but it's an important step in owning your convictions and allowing the Spirit to lead you into deeper intimacy with Him. I pray that you enjoy this book and that it becomes a blessing to you and your family

Chapter 1: Pain Becoming a Platform

Digging Deep into Memories

My personal testimony is a vital part of the reason my wife and I decided to answer God's call to the ministry of fighting against human trafficking and modern-day slavery. The first couple chapters in this book recount a part of my journey that started with pain and ended with healing that I received through a miraculous encounter with the Healer, Jesus Christ. It's a journey through my childhood into adulthood, when I learned that confronting painful memories was necessary, as it showed me how much I needed deep healing.

Many of us attempt to bury hurtful memories deep in our subconscious, without realizing that they affect our everyday decisions and, more importantly, the quality of our relationships with the people we love. I'm convicted that we do ourselves a great disservice in keeping our pain untreated; it keeps us from ever truly fulfilling our potential as God's children. It's key that we enter into a process where difficult memories can be redeemed for good. We must triumph over the evil that has plagued our lives and turn it into a blessing. When we do this, we take the weapons that the enemy has been using to torment and accuse us, and we forge them into a victorious sword that not only extinguishes the enemy's lies, but also advances God's Kingdom.

Healing requires a process we must engage in deeply, intensely, and intentionally. For me, saying a simple prayer or reciting self-help phrases wasn't enough. Neither was mindfulness. I had to enter into profound meditation and self-reflection in order to extract the deepest painful experiences of my life. I reacted both physically and emotionally to this process, which—to say the least—wasn't easy. I sought wise counsel and was given guided prayer sessions to help me through the most challenging parts of recalling pain.

The most delightful and powerful outcome of this process was really understanding myself and who God is in my life. I came to a deeper comprehension of unconditional love, incessant grace, and most importantly, God's constant presence in my life. The revelation that God was present in my darkest and most painful experiences gave me great comfort and peace. That's the most important point of this story. I don't want us to find ourselves caught in a maelstrom talking about our problems. Rather, when we actually go through proper healing, we come to know the Healer, and He's the One who completely transforms us.

Sometimes We Hide Our Memories from Ourselves

Before my parents became missionaries in South America, we led a typical immigrant life in the United States. My parents got married in South Korea and immigrated to the U.S. Almost a year after they arrived in Washington D.C., I was born. My parents worked as hard as possible in self-owned businesses to provide for our family. My grandmother was regularly in our home to watch over my younger brother and me after school. We moved around quite a bit, always looking for a bigger house and a better school district.

Finally, we moved into a townhouse in Chantilly, Virginia, where I made new friends in our neighborhood, played in the forest until I was filthy, and swam in the community pool on hot summer days. Eventually, after I left home for college, my parents moved to Paraguay to do missionary work.

I learned how deep we can bury suffering into our subconscious during my college years, after I started dating my wife, Janice. We started talking about our childhoods to get to know each other. I was baffled when Janice told me about her first day of school, her second-grade teacher, and the classmates she had while growing up. I had thought it was impossible to remember those events, since I had no memories of them myself. I couldn't even remember my teachers' names or the faces of the classmates who sat beside me all school-year long.

I assumed Janice had an impeccable memory, until I started asking my other friends how much they remembered about their past and found out they remembered as much as Janice did. The question even seemed to puzzle them. Was I the only one who had a blank memory? Why were there so many dark spots in my childhood?   In a moment of introspection, I realized that my memories became crystal clear after we moved out of the townhouse in Chantilly, halfway through my fourth-grade year. I started to wonder why I couldn't remember anything before then. Suddenly, it made sense. Something had happened in that townhouse to significantly scar me.

Innocence Robbed

When I was eight years old, my mother hired Greg, our neighbor's high school son, to be my cello instructor. He played in his school orchestra and his parents were upstanding members in our community. They seemed like a trustworthy family, and I spent many afternoons at their house alone with Greg. Greg made a great impression on me. I thought highly of him and saw his family as the epitome of the "American Dream." One afternoon, my relationship with Greg took a strange, dark turn.

First, he began to tell me about his sex life with his girlfriend, which was awkward for me as a young child. Then, he told me to undress. Greg sexually abused and raped me that day, and multiple other times. He made me promise not to tell anyone what happened between us. To make matters worse, playtime with other children in that neighborhood was frequently overtly sexual, and we'd often end up naked in bed with each other. It's clear to me now that I wasn't the only child there who was a victim of sexual abuse.

These experiences left me confused and ashamed. Moreover, I kept my word to Greg and didn't tell anyone about what happened to me. I didn't tell the other kids in the neighborhood, and I definitely didn't tell my parents. I thought I would get in trouble if I did. At the time, silence seemed to be the best way to cope with the shame I felt. Consequently, I buried my shame and memories deep in my past and never dealt with them directly. I lived out the rest of my childhood and adolescence negating these horrific

Painful Miracles

experiences, secretly hoping they would eventually go away without ever really affecting me.

The Power of Redeemed Pain

Uncovering pain from our past can be an uncomfortable process. We may end up reliving moments that caused hurt, regrets, bitterness, and anger. However, if we leave painful memories buried, they will still eventually find their way out of their hiding place. They show up in our tendencies, fears, and the inner vows we make throughout our lives. This is not the type of life God intended for us. We need to be free of this burden.

My experience with sexual abuse shattered my self-esteem. In my early adulthood, most everything I did as a husband, father, and ministry leader was to quench the burning shame that infected my self-image. This dysfunction affected most of my close relationships with family and friends. I was always trying to prove my worth to others, and I intensely longed for verbal affirmations to soothe thoughts about my own worthlessness. I did therapy sessions with psychologists, but they only taught me to manage my pain instead of truly healing from it.

This process of pain management went on for years, during which time I made an inner vow to do everything in my power to prevent my children from being abused. When we make vows like this one, we often become full of fear and dysfunction. In my case, I was constantly paranoid that something was going to happen to my children. This wasn't how I wanted to live my life, but I still felt caged in by my fears. I felt as if this was the only way to maintain any sanity or control.

Things began to shift for me when I started to learn about human trafficking. I was enraged and indignant about the fact that millions of children throughout the world are raped every night. I asked God how He could let this happen. Doesn't He care about the young and the innocent? As I cried out for justice, God threw me a curveball. Loudly and clearly, He said, "Benny, you didn't go through your pain just to protect your children. You went through that pain so that it can become a platform to show My power to the world."

I was surprised by such a paradoxical statement, but it also made sense to me. My painful experiences weren't intended for me alone. Yes, they were mine, but I had to do something more with them than just vow to protect my children. I also knew I'd need more than my own experiences to fuel a passion for hurting people, because empathy on its own was not going to make my pain a platform for God's power.

In addition, I'd need more than transparency with others about what I had gone through as a child, because being an open book for others wouldn't be enough either. I'd need to take a further step. I'd need to surrender my pain to God and allow Him to heal it, to rescue back everything that had been stolen from me, and to bless myself and my abuser. I know that's a lot to swallow at once. My process has taken years, but it's been necessary so that God can take my pain and make it a platform. The first step was to say, "Yes, Lord, whatever You want to do with my life, go ahead. My life is yours." That's when my journey to fight human trafficking began.

Redeeming pain begins with complete surrender and obedience. I wish it first came with clarity and understanding, but that's not how I've seen God work throughout the years. He looks for you to say "yes" before He reveals details. If you're ready, pause for a moment now and simply say, "Yes, Lord."

Steps towards Forgiveness

There are steps we need to take to heal our pain. For me, I needed to forgive my abuser. You may need to forgive those who hurt you, too. I believe that saying, "I forgive you" is just the beginning of the healing process, not the end. After that, we need to surrender our pain to God, because He wants to rescue us from all affliction. Not a lot of people talk about forgiveness as a step towards healing, and it might be a new concept for you. You may find yourself holding on to pain and wondering why you feel such deep bitterness and resentment. This happens when we skip important steps of our healing process with God. I encourage you to surrender your pain to Jesus now. Remember that He cares deeply for you, understands your affliction, and embraces you.

Once you've surrendered your pain, you need to rescue back everything that has been stolen from you. In my case, I had to rescue back childlike innocence and sexual purity. The truth is that I once possessed innocence and purity. Being abused robbed those from me, but they were originally mine.

I encourage you to go beyond forgiveness and surrender, towards rescuing back everything that was stolen from you as a result of your painful experiences. You may have lived a lifetime with a distorted self-image, but it's now time to reclaim what God placed within you when He formed you. Take hold of all the things that were stolen by writing them down and prayerfully proclaiming that you are their rightful owner. Cancel all the lies the enemy used against you while you lacked these characteristics and qualities. In contrast to all the lies you have believed, proclaim the truth over yourself. I did this by saying, "I am innocent, and I am pure." These words of blessing negated the curses I experienced from pain.

After blessing yourself, you can also bless those who cursed you. I know this might seem like a foreign concept, but it's a crucial step in closing the circle of complete forgiveness. I personally had to bless my abuser with a fruitful life, a solid marriage and family, and a healthy sexual lifestyle. Doing this was liberating, because I no longer saw Greg as an abuser. Instead, I began to see him as a broken individual who needed God's grace and mercy. I also stopped being a perpetual victim and got to a position in which I could freely bless someone who caused me deep pain and suffering.

Forgiving my abuser, rescuing back what he stole from me, and blessing myself and him allowed me to find redemption in my pain. It was no longer an experience that caused me to react in sorrow; it became a strength. I am now able to share my story without bitterness and draw from it to help others. I can act in true compassion, free from the weight of past pain.   My experiences are now almost a superpower, allowing me to connect openly with people and pursue justice holistically.

I bless you now to take the steps described in this chapter and to walk in the freedom of complete and total forgiveness.   As you do this, I impart redemption to you in your pain, to the point that it becomes your greatest strength. May this journey lead you to connect and bless others with your story so that they, too, may find freedom in their lives.

Chapter 2: Your Scars Are Your Testimony

A Road Trip Gone Wrong

When we've gone through trauma, we often end up with scars from our wounds. Some are physical scars and many are emotional ones. Scars are not considered "pretty," so we tend to hide them. Because they are a reminder of a painful past, we usually find ways to cover them up. However, all scars have a story to tell. The scars I have on my left forearm tell the story of a miraculous healing.

It was the first year of our ministry fighting human trafficking, and we were back in California raising support and funds for the safe home we had opened for sexually exploited minors. I was especially excited about this trip, because I was given the rare opportunity to share with our home church about our ministry. I was expecting to engage our U.S. church community in our social justice endeavors in Mexico City. In retrospect, I was proudly thinking to myself, "This is my moment to gain recognition." Nothing turned out the way I expected.

Four days before I was supposed to share at our church, we decided to visit family in the Inland Empire, about an hour and a half east of Los Angeles. As we began our trip, we realized my wife, our two kids, and I couldn't all fit into our car, so I got on my motorcycle and followed them to our destination. The sun and hot air were beating down on me the entire ride that summer day. Upon our arrival, I noticed that my rear tire was tread bare, so I took the bike to a local shop to replace the tire. I distinctly remember the technician telling me, "Go easy, because the tire is gonna be slippery until it breaks in." I thought to myself, "I've been riding long enough; I know what I'm doing."

As evening approached, we decided to head back to my mother-in-law's house. My wife said to me, "It's getting dark, so make sure that you stay close behind us. I want to be able to see you all the way home." I thought again to myself, "I've been riding long enough; I know what I'm doing."

About five minutes after hitting the freeway, I suddenly remembered that I had left my cellphone charger behind, so I took the next exit to go back and pick it up. I had no way of letting my wife know, so I just pulled a maverick move and decided that it was better to retrieve my cellphone charger than do as my wife asked. Note to all husbands reading this: *Always* listen to your wife.

Once I was back on the freeway, I felt great about myself and settled into the long ride home. After about 30 minutes, I started to feel drowsy. Realizing the heat of the day had waned on me, I knew I was going to have to fight to stay alert. As soon as that thought crossed my mind, I saw the freeway interchange I needed to take and, noticing I was about to pass it, swung my motorcycle hard to the right to catch the on-ramp. In doing so, I crossed over a part of the painted median where gravel was spread all over the pavement. That's when everything went very wrong.

Due to a combination of my fatigue, speed, the gravel on the pavement, and a brand new, slick rear tire, I started to swerve and fishtail uncontrollably. I immediately thought,

"This is it. I'm going to die." I decided to give into the thought and said to myself, "Here I come, Jesus!" (My wife has since repeated that I should've prayed, "Jesus, save me! I have a wife and two kids!")

I lost control of the bike, it fell over on its right, my head smashed into the pavement, and I lost consciousness. I was wearing a helmet, but it was not a Department of Transportation certified helmet that supposedly provides real protection in accidents. My helmet was a dinky novelty open-face helmet that I wore to look cool. Today, I tell all motorbike riders not to repeat my vain stupidity but wear a good, Department of Transportation certified helmet.

As I regained consciousness, I saw bright lights from behind my closed eyes and heard talking around me. I thought to myself, "Could this be… Heaven?" Much to my dismay, as I peeled open my swollen eyes, I saw a paramedic hovering over me and realized I was in an ambulance being taken away from the scene of the accident. My next thought was, "Oh no, I'm not dead! Now I'm in real big trouble with my wife." When the paramedic noticed I was awake, he began to ask me questions. I remained conscious long enough to tell him that I knew I had been in an accident and to relay a phone number for them to contact my family. The last thing I remember from laying in the ambulance is feeling shocked that the pant legs of my favorite pair of jeans were being cut.

I came to again when they took me off the stretcher and put me on a metal table to scan my body. The cold temperature of the table woke me from my drug-induced slumber. As I laid almost motionless while going through the scanner, I thought, "Boy…this is NOT good." Then I blacked out again.

Next, I remember hearing my wife's voice as she walked into the emergency room with the doctor. I opened my eyes long enough to see her faint from seeing my condition. I knew I probably looked *really* bad. The swelling on my head was so intense it looked like I was growing a cantaloupe out of its side.

A couple hours later, I had fully regained consciousness, and the emergency room doctor came to speak with me. He asked a series of questions to see how coherent I was, and much to my approval, I answered everything correctly. Then the bad news came. The doctor informed me that I had multiple fractures in my face and cranium, road rash on the right side of my face, hemorrhaging in my brain, and a broken left forearm. He let me know that I was "lucky" to be alive, that I would need surgery and then six to eight weeks in the hospital to recover. My heart sank.

"Doc, I can't be stuck here for six to eight weeks. I have to be at church on Sunday!" I said. I was overwhelmed with gloom as I realized that I wouldn't be able to share at church and that we didn't have any medical insurance. I had no clue how we were going to pay for all these medical bills. Eyes filled with tears, I looked over to my wife and was only able to utter, "I'm so sorry, honey. I messed up."

Can Something Good Come from this Mess?

By morning, Janice had contacted as many people as she could to intercede for us. Our church family spread the news on social media and people started calling to see if they could visit us. One of the visitors we had in the early afternoon was Janice's cousin and her husband, Ann and John Hansen, the family that we were visiting the day before. John Hansen is the lead pastor at Centerpoint Church in Murrieta, California. He is an amazing leader and a faith-filled Godly man.

He brought oil to anoint my forehead, and everyone in the room began to pray for me. Suddenly, something extraordinary happened: I started to feel the bones in my face and head shift and move. At first, I thought it was an effect of the morphine I'd been given, but then I realized it was much more than that. God was healing me! After they finished praying, there wasn't a noticeable difference in my appearance. Later in the afternoon, when I was alone in my hospital room, I decided to get up and wash my face. When I looked in the mirror, I saw that my face and head were almost back to normal size.

As I ran water over the scabs on my face, they fell off, revealing fresh, new skin underneath. The doctors ran scans and were completely perplexed as they reported to me that they could not find any fractures or hemorrhaging. The only injury I still had was a broken left forearm. They decided to keep me overnight for observation, but by Friday morning—since I could have surgery on my forearm at an out-patient facility—I was released from hospital care. Around 1:30 P.M. on a Friday afternoon, I walked out of the hospital on my own two feet. I didn't even accept a wheelchair, because I was afraid of being charged for it.

I was ecstatic to be healed, but all too quickly, the reality of hospital bills set in. All of the fees plus the cost of surgery for my left forearm came to a grand total of around 30 thousand dollars. Even though I was experiencing a miracle, I was also facing a seemingly insurmountable financial burden. Our family had given up medical insurance to cut costs and embrace full-time ministry, so we had no way of paying these expensive bills. (As a matter of fact, medical expenses are still something we leave completely in the Father's hands today.) I was immediately filled with deep regret and hopelessness. Isn't it interesting that sometimes when we overcome one challenge, we have another one waiting for us right around the corner? The silver lining of this mess was that I was able to make it to church.

I arrived to church that Sunday with my left arm in a sling. People who had so kindly visited me in the hospital in the days before were absolutely astonished at my recovery. They couldn't believe their eyes. I was feeling a bit anxious during the service, knowing that the moment to share about the anti-trafficking work we were doing was coming up, and we needed donations to get us through our next season in ministry. Our pastor, Dave Gibbons, invited me up on stage after the church announcements and stood by me the whole time I was sharing about our nonprofit, El Pozo de Vida. His presence on stage with me that day felt like that of an entire army. A supernatural sense of confidence overtook me as I spoke, knowing that I was exactly where God wanted me to be, doing exactly what He wanted me to do.

After the offering baskets were passed around, Dave turned to me and asked, "Benny, could you please share with us why your arm is in a sling? What happened to you this week?" I began to share with the congregation about my accident and how God had healed me, and an intense silence filled the room. Afterwards, Dave turned towards the people with a smile on his face and said, "You know, Benny and his family have sacrificed a lot to be in Mexico. Right now, they don't have any medical insurance to pay their hospital bills. They're part of our church family, so would you please consider giving again to help them cover their medical expenses?"

I felt my knees go weak and tears fill my eyes at this unexpected act of kindness towards us. I immediately turned to Dave, gave him a one-arm hug, and thanked him with the deepest amount of gratitude I could express. After leaving the stage, my body returned to my seat, but my head was flying high. It was the strangest feeling.

That same afternoon, I received a call from the church's executive pastor. He said to me, "Benny, I'm calling to let you know that we counted the offerings for your medical expenses and we collected 30 thousand dollars to help you meet this need." Crazy! Absolutely bonkers! All I could do was thank God over and over again for His faithfulness in our lives. Later, we were told by a couple of church members that the Holy Spirit had told them to take lots of cash to church that day. When they heard about our financial situation, they knew that was why they needed to have brought that money.

Your Scars Can Be a Testimony

Remember how I also broke my left forearm in my accident? Those bones weren't miraculously healed from the prayer I received. I sometimes joke that it could be because Pastor John only laid his hands on my head and never on my forearm. All joking aside, I had surgery, and plates were screwed into the bones of my left forearm, leaving me with two massive scars. I believe that I needed a couple of scars as proof of what God did in my life. To this day, I am constantly asked about the story behind my scars, and I have the chance to proudly hold up my arm and tell people how God did a miracle in my life. It was a painful one, to say the least, but it left me with an amazing story to share.

What scars do you have, and have you been covering them up? Even if you didn't experience a healing or a miracle at the time of your suffering, God can still turn your scars into something beautiful. Just like He did with the abuse that I suffered, God can radically redeem your dark memories and transform your hurt into a great strength. I encourage you to surrender your pain.

Close your eyes with your hands out and palms open. Prayerfully visualize yourself surrendering all of the heaviness and hurt from your painful experiences to the Lord. Stay in this moment until you are certain you've emptied your hands of your burden. Now that your hands are empty, ask God to fill them with what He intends for you. Remember that God is good, merciful, and compassionate towards us. His intentions for us are for our benefit.

It may help to remember Joseph's story in the book of Genesis. Joseph was betrayed by his brothers, sold into slavery, falsely accused, and put in jail by Potiphar's wife. In a turn of wild events, Joseph interpreted the pharaoh's dreams and was put in charge of the Egyptian empire, second only to the pharaoh himself. After many years, Joseph got to face his brothers again, and when his brothers begged him for mercy, Joseph said:

> Don't be afraid of me. Am I God, that I can punish you? You intended to harm me, but God intended it all for good. He brought me to this position so I could save the lives of many people (Gen. 50:19b-20).

Joseph's story should give you confidence to know that even though you may have faced a great deal of trials, God can use them to bless many people if you surrender your pain and allow Him to fill your destiny with His loving intentions. As you begin to receive from the Lord now, open your ears to hear what He has to say to you.

People always ask me how we can know that God is speaking to us. To me, God's voice sounds louder than a whisper, but quieter than normal speaking volume. I hear His voice in my heart, not in my head. Regardless of how you may hear God's voice, He will definitely speak words of blessing and encouragement. It's important for you to receive these words with an open heart. I suggest that you say out loud, "I receive these words." By doing so, you verbally declare affirmation and acceptance of God's words of blessing and encouragement. This step is important for the words to begin to take root in your life, grow, and eventually bear fruit.

It's up to you to start living out the blessings and promises God has spoken over your life. Contrary to popular belief, it doesn't always automatically or magically happen. You have to do your part by taking tangible steps in making the words a reality for you. This is your act of trust and obedience. My personal process involved taking steps to fight human trafficking, which eventually led my wife and I to start two successful nonprofit organizations. This process was arduous but worth it. Today, I feel like I am living out God's dream for me, as well as thoroughly enjoying my life. It's dark at times, but it's always fun to see God's Kingdom invade and conquer the evil that is in this world.

I encourage you to write down the next steps that you want to take. You can even imagine where you will be five to ten years in the future. I did this exercise over ten years ago, and I believe we accomplished in ten years what I thought we could only accomplish in 20. I'm not boasting. It was only through God's grace that we got to where we are today. I believe that testimonies give us power to walk in God's destiny for us. Be encouraged and take tangible steps today. I know that God has an adventure waiting for you.

Chapter 3: Seek the Healer, Not the Healing

Trying to Understand the Scope of the Problem

Our local nonprofit in Mexico City currently runs over ten projects in three key focus areas to fight human trafficking, creating a holistic approach necessary for significant impact in this complex issue. The focus areas are prevention, intervention, and restoration. We often use an allegory to explain how this works:

> Imagine yourself walking alone next to a rushing river in a forest. As you walk, you begin to hear a baby crying and notice that the baby is floating in a basket down the river. What do you do?

> Hopefully, you decide to jump in the river and save the baby. Now, once you've jumped in, saved the baby from the river's unknown perils, and moved her/him to dry ground, you hear another baby in a basket floating down the river. You jump in to save that baby, but then you hear yet another baby. You realize there's a seemingly unending flow of helpless babies floating down this rushing river. What questions pop into your head?

> Most likely you'll wonder, "Where are the babies coming from and where are they going? Who can help me rescue these babies? And what am I going to do with all of the babies that I've rescued from the river?"

The task of walking upstream to try and stop the problem before it starts, which includes understanding what's causing the babies to be thrown into the river, is the work of prevention. It's about preventing the problem, preventing innocent people from having to suffer pain or put themselves at any risk. Doing so also makes the job of the people working downstream a lot easier.

Preventing human trafficking can look like awareness campaigns that are specifically designed for a target audience who may be at risk of being trafficked. Our nonprofit focuses on middle and high school youth, because statistics show that around the world, the average age people become victims of a human trafficking scheme is between 13 and 15 years old. Educating youth to understand the tactics a trafficker may use to lure them into a vulnerable situation is essential in helping them detect when they or a friend could fall into a trafficker's hands. It's also important to take the same message to parents and teachers, so that if they see signs that a child is in danger of becoming a trafficking victim, they can intervene in a timely fashion.

Preventing human trafficking also includes addressing the demand for it. It's not enough to reduce the number of factors that contribute to people becoming victims of human trafficking. Efforts must be made to curb the demand for sexual exploitation, with the intent of eliminating it altogether. Looking at prevention through the lens of supply and demand can seem dehumanizing, but a macro-level perspective helps us develop strategic initiatives.

For example, our nonprofit recently launched an anti-machismo campaign, which included a thought-provoking video, a social media challenge, and online discussion groups about masculinity and machismo. We did this to address one of the root causes of human trafficking buried deep in cultural norms. We understand that the root of sexual exploitation is gender violence, the root of gender violence is gender inequality, and the root of gender inequality is cultural norms like machismo. Our campaign reached over 20 million people.

Jumping into the river to rescue the floating babies is intervention work. Intervention is reaching victims when they are at-risk and vulnerable in order to lead them to safety. Many people assume that intervention in human trafficking is like a rescue movie scene in which someone kicks down the doors of a brothel, grabs the damsel in distress from the grips of a trafficker, and escapes to safety.

A real rescue actually consists of much more than that. First, intervention teams meet victims where they are at. This is why most of our organization's intervention programs are in the heart of the red-light district. When we do this, it's important to let go of any presuppositions we have of victims, because we do not want prejudice to misguide us in engaging with them. We also try not to say that we empower our beneficiaries, because that implies we have power to give. Rather, we say that we walk alongside our beneficiaries in their own process of empowerment.

Intervention is more than physically removing people from a geographical location. This work must address the emotional and spiritual chains that keep a person in bondage. Certain mindsets or beliefs may have caused individuals to make poor or self-destructive decisions, keeping them entangled in their chains. Intervention involves helping victims believe in themselves until they believe they can be free from the bonds of human trafficking.

Lastly, caring for the babies after they are taken out of the river is the goal of restoration, a critical piece to our holistic model. In human trafficking, restoration is the long and arduous process of helping survivors in their process of physical and emotional healing, as well as their process of reintegration into society. It's a marathon, not a sprint. We have the most experience in this stage because our safe house was our nonprofit's first program. As we grew, we saw the need for additional services beyond those we were already providing through safe shelter, psychological therapy, and education. Our beneficiaries needed vocational training, job placement assistance, and even employment within our organization. We also opened two transition homes for girls who age out of our safe house, which has a staged approach involving a gradual and individualized path towards independence.

This holistic approach allows us to journey alongside our beneficiaries as they move from being victims (or avoid becoming victims) to successfully reintegrating into society. Since human trafficking is systemic, it requires systematized strategies to address all aspects of it. We have to find a way to reach everyone, whether they are in danger of falling into the river, are floating down it, have already been rescued out of it, or are contributing to throwing people into it. In other words, we need prevention, intervention, and restoration. We must go beyond assistentialism, philanthropy, and charity; beyond watching, giving, and donating; beyond primarily addressing immediate needs. To really end this global injustice, we must also help change culture.

No Fault of Her Own

In the early years of our safe house project, we received a teenage girl from southern Mexico. To protect her identity, we will call her by a fictitious name, Sandra. Sandra had been approached by a woman, a family friend, who promised her work in Mexico City. She thought to herself, "I can make good money working in the big city to help support my family financially." After talking it over with her parents, she left home for what seemed like an amazing opportunity and adventure. When she arrived in the city, things took a turn for the worst.

Sandra's family friend used a standard tactic of human traffickers for luring potential victims: preying on the vulnerable and weak. Traffickers are aware when certain regions and populations are struggling financially, and they approach vulnerable people and paint them a beautiful picture of prosperity and financial stability. More importantly, they look for emotional vulnerability: young girls from broken families, with absentee parental figures, who long for attention and self-worth. This type of vulnerability can just as easily describe an affluent girl from the city as it can describe a girl from a socio-economically marginalized region. Traffickers do not limit their sourcing to small and rural towns. The push and pull factors for victims of human trafficking are not merely socio-economic in nature. Traffickers are drawn to those who are emotionally vulnerable, because it allows them to create a bond with their victims that is stronger than bonds with merely economically vulnerable victims.

Deconstructing the Blame Game

Creating emotional bondage increases the chances of enslaving a person. This is why I strongly believe that healthy families can end human trafficking. If our daughters grow up knowing their self-worth and identity in Christ, surrounded by healthy and solid family values, they won't need to seek attention from people who could potentially prey on their weaknesses. Do you ever wonder why young girls take so many selfies? Are they crying out for attention and approval from men? Why do they feel a need to show off their bodies in sexually enticing ways?

Healthy families are equally as important in raising young men who view girls and women as precious to God, not as sexual objects to be used for their viewing or physical pleasure. If parents raise their boys to respect and honor girls, we can end the demand for sex trafficking and pornography in the next generation.

At times, we oversimplify the problem by playing the "blame game" and wholly condemning those we perceive as causing human trafficking rather than accepting our own responsibility to form healthy families. We are quick to point our fingers at victims, traffickers, and consumers, when we should examine ourselves instead to see where we may have failed to establish Kingdom culture. Let's stop simply blaming victims and their families for being blinded by financial circumstances. Let's stop simply denigrating traffickers for being hopeless, evil criminals. Let's stop simply judging consumers of sex services for thoughtlessly partaking in systemic injustice.

I agree that we should address macro socio-economic issues and seek full legal punishment for those who prey on the weak; however, causality is not responsibility. We must clearly separate the two. For example, when we presuppose that poverty is one of the main causes of human trafficking, we cannot in the same breath state that poor families are solely responsible for their socio-economic status. When we have a holistic perspective of the systems that cause poverty and other social injustices, we realize that we all have a responsibility to maintain a just society. We are responsible for establishing strong values and self-worth in our families and communities. We are responsible for raising up a generation that values the image of God in every human being. If we all own up to our responsibilities, we can shape the course of future generations and bring freedom to all who are enslaved.

Back to Sandra's Story

Sandra arrived in Mexico City with her family friend thinking that in a few short days, she would start a new job to help financially support her family. She got off the bus full of hope, left the bus terminal, and was then sold to two men. They stripped her naked, raped her, and chained her to the floor in a small concrete room that had no flooring or furniture. She tried to fight back but was repeatedly beaten by the men who were trying to subdue her. She was given to be used by men up to 30 times a day and continuously physically abused. Eventually, her fighting spirit was broken.

After a couple months of this nightmare, the two men put her on the street to work as a prostitute. She had become so full of fear and shame that she didn't run away but did exactly what she was told to.

This is what modern-day slavery looks like. Many of us see young women or men on street corners and think that they may be working out of their own free will or for financial reasons, when in fact, we don't know what they went through to be in their current position. We don't know what may have died inside them, keeping them captive. They may not have physical chains, but the emotional chains they bear are far heavier than any physical ones ever could be.

Thankfully, Sandra was seen by someone who believed she looked too young to be in prostitution and reported the case to the authorities, who ran a sting operation and rescued this teenage girl. They contacted us, and we took Sandra into our safe house, where she slowly began her process of restoration. Soon after arriving, she began to complain that she was hard of hearing. We took her to a specialist who confirmed that she had lost 100% of her hearing in one ear and 50% in the other as a result of the abuse she had suffered. We were able to get her a hearing aid for the ear that still had some hearing left to improve her quality of life and allow her to continue her education.

Seek the Healer, Not the Healing

One Friday afternoon, a few months into her time at the safe house, Sandra asked what it's like to hear God's voice. After we explained it to her, she asked us to pray for her to hear God's voice. Nothing miraculous happened in the moment, but her heart was seeking God. The next morning, the other girls at the safe house woke up early and were being obnoxiously loud in the main patio area. Since the girls are allowed to sleep in on Saturdays, Sandra burst out of her room asking them to keep the noise down, because she was trying to sleep. Suddenly, she noticed she was not wearing her hearing aid, as she had taken it off the night before. She exclaimed to our staff, "I don't have my hearing aid in and I can hear!" Unconvinced, our staff told her we would take her to see hearing specialists first thing Monday morning.

The hearing specialists ran a series of tests. Perplexed by the results, they thought their machine was malfunctioning. They pulled out another testing machine and ran tests for over two hours. That day, Sandra received a diagnosis of 100% restored hearing in both ears. It was a miracle! A doctor friend of mine was visiting at the time and couldn't believe what he was hearing. Wanting to examine Sandra's ears himself, he took out his otoscope and looked into them. In disbelief, he said, "Benny, I don't know what to tell you. I can still see the damage from the trauma to her ear. There is no way to medically explain how she can hear." This proved that Sandra's hearing wasn't restored through a physically restorative miracle, which is what I thought had happened. From that moment on and to this day, Sandra hears supernaturally!

Remember, Sandra never asked for this miracle; she only wanted to hear God's voice. She didn't seek the healing; she sought the Healer. This was an important lesson for me, and one we should all learn. Always seek intimacy with God first because everything else flows out of that relationship. We spend so much time seeking provision, healing, and rescue, when we should be focusing on seeking the Provider, the Healer, and the Rescuer. Our focus needs to change from receiving something as a result of our pursuit to finding complete satisfaction and fulfillment in our relationship with God.

Focus on Intimacy with God

What would our lives look like if Jesus' intimacy with the Father were really our model? What if we threw out success, effectiveness, and impact, and traded them for deep and significant communion with our Father in Heaven? Asking myself this question, I have been learning not to focus so much on my results, but to focus instead on who the results are for. I am trying to ignore what the world considers to be success and be ruthlessly intent on hearing God's voice. You might want to try this, too. Whatever you are facing right now, I challenge you to seek the Healer and not the healing.

Seek the Kingdom of God above all else, and live righteously, and he will give you everything you need. (Matt. 6:33).

I bless you right now with a change of mindset. May you no longer be captivated by the temptation of results or success. Rather, may your heart and affections be turned towards the Father's heart. May you long to mirror God's compassion and goodness rather than to receive an answer to prayer. May the answer to your prayers be that you get to pray and commune with our Heavenly Father. Everything else will flow from that place of intimacy with Him.

Chapter 4: It's Party Time!

Creative Extremism

After a couple of years doing anti-trafficking ministry in Mexico, our influence began to expand into different countries. One of the first countries we saw open to our work was Brazil. The 2014 World Cup in Brazil was fast approaching and, shortly afterwards, the Summer Olympic Games were going to take place in Rio de Janeiro. The world's eyes would be on Brazil for the next couple of years. We formed a team in Brazil and started to raise funds to support a future anti-trafficking nonprofit that we were going to establish. In addition, we started developing methodologies to directly combat sex trafficking during large sporting events.

By the way, the jury is still out on whether or not large sporting events cause increases in sex trafficking. Most people believe that a larger, typically male pool of potential consumers traveling far from home attracts traffickers looking to increase their income. Others claim that statistics show the opposite effect. Regardless, I learned through conversations with women in situations of prostitution and sex trafficking that the commercial sex industry makes specific plans as a direct response to a surge in potential clients.

For the upcoming World Cup, we knew we had to take aggressive action to bring light into darkness and to find tangible ways to disrupt the sex-trafficking industry. Our hearts were even more deeply pained after researching for a documentary we filmed, when we discovered that children as young as eight years old were being sold for sex in Brazil. How were we going to be able to make a difference? How could innocence be saved and rescued? How were we going to stop the demand?

I wanted to think of ways to penalize and lock up traffickers and consumers. I came up with an idea to bring shame and financial consequences to them. The plan was to use cameras and lights to expose clients picking up women off the streets and follow them with cameras to their hotel entrance or wherever their destination was. The footage would be livestreamed on a website to bring public shame to these clients. When I shared my "genius" idea with wise counselors, they asked me if this method would faithfully show God's love and mercy to the people involved. I wasn't prepared for that response, nor was I prepared to think about traffickers or consumers in that way. In my heart, I knew the right thing to do was to show mercy and grace, to find a way to bless and not curse them.

I've learned throughout my years working in this field that everyone is broken in one way or another. Our place is never to judge. As a matter of fact, God never called us to judge people, because that's His job and not ours. As God's people, we have been called to love as Christ loved us. In my initial idea of shaming clients, I lost sight of God's heart for all humanity. I prioritized the goal of stopping the commercial sex industry over the path of repentance that God wants to lead us into by showing us His kindness. My focus was on the end goal, and I was willing to use any means to get there. I wasn't considering human brokenness and our need for a merciful Father.

Shortly after listening to this wise counsel, I went on a trip to Panama as part of our preparations for Brazil. It was there that we drastically changed the focus of our intervention work. Our time there showed us a path to demonstrate love without any conditions or strings attached. We went to a leadership conference hosted by an international missionary organization in Panama City. I have a lot of respect for all the radical evangelism work that this organization does around the world. They are truly inspiring and have positively shaped my personal experience with missions and evangelism.

At the conference, I had an opportunity to meet with key Brazilian leaders of this organization to talk about the outreach work they were planning for the upcoming World Cup. They had a particular interest in addressing the issue of demand for prostitution during fan festivities. I asked about their action plan, and they told me it was to go where fans gather to hand out pamphlets and talk to people about the issue of trafficking. Although this plan was solid, it lacked the direct intervention necessary to curb demand in red-light districts. I suggested conducting outreach directly with potential clients and sex workers in red-light districts, but they thoughtfully rejected the idea because of potential risk to their team members. The obvious risk was dangerous pimps intent on protecting their territory, but they also didn't want to expose their team members to sexual temptation while interacting with sex workers.

Although I understood their concerns, I was discouraged as I felt the need was too great to play it safe. More importantly, I firmly believe that we are the salt and light of the earth who have been given divine authority to shine Christ's light in the darkest, most evil places. The power of Christ's light can easily overcome any threats or temptations that may present themselves. I believe that when we face opposition to God's power, no matter how great it is, it will eventually bow its knee in submission to God's ultimate authority.

After my conversation with these Brazilian leaders, I had a decision to make. I could have chosen to give up on trying to do any anti-trafficking work in Brazil and just go back home to Mexico City. It would have been an easy decision and one that most people wouldn't have judged me for. It would have been justifiable, because Brazil is a totally different context from Mexico, and we didn't have any active ministries there. I didn't, though. I had a deep sense of conviction that pushed me past rational logic towards a place of radical faith. That place is not comfortable and everything doesn't work itself out smoothly there. When you're in the place of radical faith, you have to struggle and fight for your convictions. There are obstacles and opposition, but it's also where you are thrust forward to live out your destiny.

Running with Your Wolf Pack

Diego Traverso is a crazy, Godly Chilean man and amazing filmmaker whom I am honored to call my friend. We have traveled the world together serving in many different areas, including aiding victims of human trafficking, natural disasters, and other types of crises. Throughout the years, he has challenged me to be more creative in the ways we serve those who are in need.

Diego was with me on the trip to Panama. After our meeting with the Brazilian leaders of the international missionary organization, I turned to him and said with conviction, "We can't expect to do the type of direct outreach we envision in Brazil if we don't do it first in Mexico." He agreed, and we started to make plans.

He mentioned to me that right by his apartment in Mexico, there was a red-light district where we should start. I told him about my idea of putting on a block party to show love to sex workers, clients, and even pimps. Diego suggested a perfect group to serve as volunteers at the party and offered to film the entire evening as a way to share this testimony and document a replicable model that could be used in other areas.

Relationships like the one I have with Diego are essential. They go beyond serving or working together. There is a catalytic component to them that moves Heaven and earth. You can see examples of friendships like this throughout the Bible: David and Jonathan, Paul and Silas, Elijah and Elisha, among many others. Throughout the years, my friendship with Diego grew to include others: men by the names of Josh, Rodolfo, Dan, and Christian. If you are a leader, I encourage you to look to your right and left. Notice the friends who serve with you and do life with you. If there isn't anyone around, there might be a problem. If you have people whom you love and trust, I encourage you to bring them closer and go to battle with each other.

Commit to one another as a wolf pack, sharing your vision, mutual respect, honor, and adventurous faith.

God Held Back the Rain

After Diego and I returned to Mexico City, we started to make preparations for our outreach. We got the word out for volunteers to meet us at Diego's apartment at a specific time, and we prepared a variety of activities for the evening party in the red-light district. Our plans included distributing food and drinks, handing out flowers, enjoying live music, making bracelets with children, and giving manicures to women.

I remember driving to Diego's apartment that Saturday afternoon. It was a clear summer day without a cloud in the sky. I arrived a little early to make sure that we were logistically prepared. As people began to pour into the apartment, there was only standing room left. Things started to get chaotic. Luisa, Diego's wife, got my attention and pointed outside where a thunderstorm was obviously about to start. We could see dark ominous clouds forming a wall in the sky.

What were we supposed to do at that point? We could postpone the outreach, but we already had close to 60 people waiting to go out to the streets and serve. We could wait for the rain to pass, but there was no guarantee that there would be any sex workers on the streets afterwards. We had to seize the moment and take advantage of the time we had. I jumped on a chair and began to assign people to groups and give them responsibilities. I told everyone to be ready to serve with limited time. We all prayed together and went out onto the streets.

By the time we got outside, the wind was blowing strongly. When I looked up at the sky, I could see a clear demarcation of bright blue skies and grayish-black storm clouds. Diego commented to me as he was filming, "Look above where we're standing. There are blue skies here, but where we need to go, the skies are dark."

My fair assessment of the situation was that we would have 15 to 30 minutes tops for our block party outreach before being rained out. As we crossed the main avenue towards where we were going to set up, I made my way to the front of our group and prayed out loud. I rebuked the wind and rain, claimed the power and authority of Jesus, and declared that God's unconditional love would be made evident that evening. The wind kicked up dust into my mouth as I prayed louder, shouting.

We got to the street corner and briskly set up all of our decorations. We sent groups to pass out flowers, inviting women to the festivities. Live music was playing and we began distributing food and drinks. The children in the neighborhood came out to see what was happening on the street corner. Our volunteers invited them to make bracelets and played impromptu games with them. Women started to arrive, and they received prayer and manicures. Some spontaneous dancing even broke out. It reminded of the lyrics to the song, "Did You Hear the Mountains Tremble," specifically the line about "dancers who dance upon injustice." Seeing a block party disrupt sex commerce for a moment and shine light on such a dark street corner in the city was like watching a miracle happen before our eyes.

We were so caught up in our festivities that we forgot about the impending thunderstorm. After about two and a half hours, we realized that not a single rain drop had fallen. To make the story even better, volunteers who walked home after the party reported that a couple of blocks away from us, the streets were so flooded that it was impossible to cross at some points. God held back the rain, and we got the whole thing on tape.

This experience assured us there is absolutely nothing that can hold back or detain God's love. It created a deep sense of radical boldness in us. As we looked forward to what we were planning in Brazil's red-light districts, we had full confidence that we would witness miracles every time we took Christ's light to dark streets where sex commerce was active.

Just a few months later during the World Cup in Brazil, we adapted the strategies used in our outreaches in Mexico City and conducted block parties in red-light districts in different cities all over the nation, setting a precedence for creative methods to reach vulnerable populations. Monthly block parties in Mexico and Brazil continue to take place to this day.

The bold steps we took during that first block party in Mexico taught us key lessons. The first is that we have to approach seemingly insurmountable odds with creative solutions. If the opposition is using schemes impossible to undo through standard strategies, then we must take a different approach. We must be innovative, think critically, and try non-standard approaches to address issues. I believe we can be the most creative beings in the world because we were created in the image and likeness of the Creator of the universe. It's a matter of using this part of our nature, the creativity we have from being like the Creator, to come up with innovative solutions to problems.

The second lesson we learned is that our creativity may lead us to extreme, almost outlandish, and seemingly unattainable ideas. This is just like God's love for us. His love is extreme in its nature. If we are to love people the way God asks us to, then we must seek to love as much as He does, using His example as our measure. God's love for us is extreme in its sacrifice, audacious in its grace, and eternal in its patience. What would it look like to really love others as God loves us?

Always Bless, Never Curse

"Always bless and never curse" seems like an obvious principle of practicing Christian faith. However, I want to challenge you to think about the subtle ways that we discriminate in showing kindness to others. For example, we withhold patience towards people who are in the process of becoming more like Jesus, and we judge individuals stuck in situations due to what we perceive as their own stupidity. As we hesitate to show them kindness, we make assumptions about them, usually assuming the worst. We may think that someone deserves what they are experiencing, that they had it coming. We may even think they are destined to fail. These types of thoughts are curses. We must be careful not to judge people, not even subtly.

To avoid judging, it helps me to ask people more questions about their journey. I try to allow them to tell their own stories instead of jumping to my own conclusions and telling their stories myself. It's not just about trying to put yourself in someone else's shoes. It's about giving people the freedom to share their own stories, explaining their own thoughts in their own words. I try to listen and resist my urge to superimpose my perception of a person on their identity. They must have the main voice in telling their own story, and I shouldn't interfere.

What I've found is that people just want to be heard. If you listen, your initial perceptions of someone may significantly change. I encourage you to take some time this week and allow yourself to hear someone's story without making any prior judgements about them. Give them the opportunity to tell their complete story without interruptions. I know you will be pleasantly surprised. Most likely, you'll want an opportunity to share your own story.

In addition to not cursing, we can take a step toward proactively blessing others. Let's consider the contexts of most miracles Jesus performed in the Gospel narratives. Many of the people Jesus physically healed were considered outcasts or belonged to the lower rungs of society. Lepers, the blind, and the demon-possessed received healing miracles. Sometimes we inadvertently assign contrasting amounts of value to different types of people and determine who is worthy to receive a blessing. We usually do this according to our own prejudices, the prejudices that give way for us to curse people. Jesus never withheld blessings to those whom society considered unworthy.

Jesus' miracles showed no discrimination against society's most rejected. In fact, Jesus even preferred outcasts. What would this world look like if God's people demonstrated this same principle in their daily interactions? What if the Church was known as a safe place with zero judgement and no discrimination towards others? What if we were known for being extravagant in how we bless others, always being inclusive, unconditionally embracing people, and showing great generosity? I don't mean to criticize the Church as a whole, but we all have the responsibility and opportunity to make a difference in the lives that we come into contact with every day.

Would you take some time to consider the people around you who have been rejected and then make a conscious decision to bless them? As you approach them, are you willing to forgo your presuppositions and listen to them tell their own stories on their own terms? I am almost certain that in doing so, something miraculous will happen for both of you. When we engage in acts of compassion without any prejudice, it sets the stage for an outpouring of miraculous blessings.

One of my mentors used to explain the Gospel by stretching out his hand with his palm facing down, fingers dangling, and then move his hand downwards, saying, "The Gospel is not about coming from the top down." Then, he would face the palm of his hand up, start moving it up, and say, "The Gospel is about going below and lifting up."

This simple phrase and hand motion constitute a profound thought. For centuries, religion has attempted to impose its power and will on others. Historically, religion was propagated through force, and the religious even threatened death to those who didn't comply. As Jesus' followers, we inherently have a contrasting ethos. When we carefully examine Jesus' incarnation and public ministry, we see that He exhibited humility in serving others, offering freedom and new life. We should all honestly examine how we engage with others and apply this principle of *down-up* rather than *up-down*.

If you feel rejected by society, your community, or even your family, I encourage you to prayerfully close your eyes and ask God to speak words of affirmation and encouragement to you. Recall a moment when you were rejected or felt rejected by others, then prayerfully invite Jesus into that memory, noticing His facial expressions, actions, and the words He has to say to you. I guarantee that you will only hear words that console or uplift you. If you hear anything else, the words may be your own or accusations from the enemy.

I did this exercise years ago and recalled the moment I was raped as a child. I could see Jesus weeping with deep compassion. I could hear His voice bringing words of healing and truth that served as a healing balm on all my wounds. Moreover, His presence in the moment of my abuse reminded me that I was never abandoned, and His promise to never leave or forsake me rings true in my heart today.

I pray that you will experience the same. I pray that you have a divine encounter where you will find healing for your deepest pain. I also pray that you will share the grace given to you with others, blessing them.

Chapter 5: Do You Want to Receive a Blessing?

An Anniversary Gift

My 15-year wedding anniversary with Janice happened to coincide with one of our visits to California, so we decided to leave our kids with family and celebrate for a couple of days in Laguna Beach. One of our friends, who heard of our plans, came up to us after a church service and said, "Do you two want to receive a blessing?" My wife and I looked at each other, smiled in agreement, and answered, "Yes, we do!" It's not every day that someone wants to bless you with a gift. Our friend said that she would arrange two nice dinners for us, calling ahead of time and paying for our meals. All we had to do was show up and eat. It sounded like an amazing plan.

The next day, we headed to Laguna Beach, curiously wondering what our dinners the next two nights would be like. We checked into our hotel and went to our first dinner destination. The place was spectacular! It had an ocean view and premier service. We felt like we were in a dream. As dessert was about to be served, I got a phone call from our generous friend. I assumed she wanted to make sure we were enjoying our evening and that everything was going fine. Instead, she said, "I'm so sorry to bother you during your dinner, but I've been trying to call the restaurant and the hotel the restaurant is in. I've used my cell phone and land lines, but I can't seem to get through. Could you please pass the phone to the manager so I can settle your bill?" I took my cell phone over to the manager, and he brought it back to me a couple minutes later. I asked him about our friend's inability to call the restaurant. He said that they weren't experiencing any problems, so the issue was mostly likely on her end. This seemed a little strange to us, but we didn't think any more of it.

The next morning, we went to a popular breakfast spot and decided to walk back to our hotel, taking the scenic route down the beach. As we walked along holding hands, taking in the warmth of the sun and coolness of the waves, we noticed our friend on the beach. We called out to her and asked, "What are you doing here? You live over an hour and a half away!" She exclaimed, "It happened again! I couldn't get through to the restaurant where you have a reservation tonight. I tried all my phones—cell phone, house phone, office phone—and none of them worked. I decided to pack up the car, bring my kids, and make a beach day of it. Don't worry; I've already taken care of everything at the restaurant. Enjoy yourselves tonight!" We told her she didn't have to drive so far to do this for us, but she was extremely generous with her time and money. As we said our goodbyes, she mentioned how she'd never had such a difficult time trying to bless someone.

Her words struck a chord in me. I remembered all the other times in our ministry when people tried to donate to our cause or bless us with gifts but faced obstacles or difficulties in doing so. I had an eerie feeling that the obstacles weren't due to natural causes; that there may be spiritual reasons people are often blocked in trying to be generous.

Generosity is a Kingdom principle. God is generous with His grace and forgiveness towards us. He is rich in mercy, and we are called to be the same way. Generosity can free us from selfish ambitions and teach us to build others up, which is why the enemy hates to see believers being generous. He uses greed and the love of money to stifle a cheerful giver, as well as leverages resentment to keep up us from being generous in our forgiveness towards others. Generosity is critical to individual freedom and Kingdom advancement, and the enemy works hard to keep it from being prevalent in the Church.

The enemy also tries hard to prevent or detain a blessing or answer to prayer from ever being received by believers. In John 10:10, Jesus mentions that He desires to give us all abundant life, but right before that, He says that the thief comes to steal, kill, and destroy. What is the thief stealing from us? We may be unaware of this, but the enemy schemes to steal our blessings and answered prayers, intending to discourage us and make us question God's love for us.

What if the thief could disrupt or detain answers to your prayers, then promptly sow words of doubt into your thought life? You might question whether God is really listening to you or wonder if you have done something wrong that has disqualified you from receiving an answer. We have all probably experienced these thoughts at some point in our lives, but they are lies. The thief's lies don't have much power or influence over us when everything is going well. We fall for them when he also effectively inhibits an answer to prayer from being received by us. His scheme is to sow a little doubt by whispering lies that cause us to question our self-worth and distort our beliefs about how God views us. His ultimate goal is to distort the image we have of God. As lies build up and we become more convinced of them, our perception of a loving and caring Heavenly Father becomes twisted.

The day will come when nothing will stand in the way of God's people praising Him. No fear, misconception, or distorted image will obscure our vision and we will fully see God on His throne. We will see Him in the fullness of His glory and truly know Him as He desires to be known by us. I long for that day, to see God in this way. When that day comes, we will also finally be able to see ourselves as God sees us, fully redeemed and clothed in righteousness. We will be in awe of what the Lord has done in each and every one of us.

In the meantime, while we are on this earth, we continue to battle against the enemy and his devious tactics. Rather than just taking his blows, I encourage you to have a heightened awareness of the machinations that potentially obstruct your ability to experience the abundant life you can have in Christ. If you have ever questioned why you don't see breakthrough in certain areas of your life, this next section might help you understand an important aspect of breakthroughs: how prayers are answered.

Delivery System of Answered Prayers

Let's take a close look at a series of events in the book of Daniel. In chapter nine, Daniel prays and repents for his actions and the actions of the people of Israel who were exiled in Babylon. In verse 20, while Daniel is still praying, the angel Gabriel appears to him "in swift flight." In verse 23, Gabriel explains, "As soon as you prayed, a word went out, which I have come to tell you." Daniel's prayers were being answered while he was praying. The answer was delivered swiftly and was available to Daniel as he began to pray.

Fast forward to chapter ten, the next chapter. Daniel has a revelation of an imminent war. He prays and mourns for three weeks, during which time he doesn't receive an answer from the Lord like he did in the previous chapter. After three weeks, he has a vision of an angel who explains to Daniel what has occurred.

> Then he said, "Don't be afraid, Daniel. Since the first day you began to pray for understanding and to humble yourself before your God, your request has been heard in heaven. I have come in answer to your prayer. But for twenty-one days the spirit prince of the kingdom of Persia blocked my way. Then Michael, one of the archangels, came to help me, and I left him there with the spirit prince of the kingdom of Persia" (Dan. 10:12-13).

The angel explains clearly that he had an answer to Daniel's prayers on the first day Daniel started to pray, but as the angel tried to deliver it, a battle with the Prince of Persia ensued, preventing the angel from presenting himself before Daniel. It wasn't until the archangel Michael came to his aid that the angel was able to escape and deliver the message.

It's not a coincidence that these two chapters are placed together. Twice, real concerns or issues drove Daniel to pray and mourn. Both times, not only were his prayers answered in spectacular fashion through the appearance of angels, but it's also explicitly expressed that the answers were made available immediately. The only difference between the two is that the first time, the angel arrived swiftly, but the second time, the angel was delayed because of a battle between demons and angels.

Though Daniel's experience is only a fragmental representation of the Heavenly delivery system of answers to prayers, we see here a snapshot of what happens in the spiritual realm when prayers are answered. It seems that God speaks or makes decrees on His Heavenly throne, and angelic beings are assigned to deliver His messages. Daniel's experience does not fully describe how every prayer is answered, since many other times throughout the Bible God directly speaks or God's people speak on His behalf. Nevertheless, Daniel's story helps reveal God's intentions and the enemy's schemes.

The fact that the answers to Daniel's prayers were clearly made available immediately may reveal that God's intention is to answer our prayers promptly. Although Daniel was a prophet referred to by angels as "highly esteemed," we shouldn't assume that his experience was exclusive to him. The Bible is clear that God does not show favoritism (Rom. 2:11). Furthermore, Jesus said that our Heavenly Father desires to give "good gifts to those who ask Him" (Matt. 7:11).

On my anniversary trip with my wife, I took all this into consideration as I reflected on the obstacles our friend faced when trying to bless us with delicious dinners to help us celebrate our marriage. It was peculiar that she exclaimed, "Why is it so hard to bless you guys?" Could our friend's phone calls to the restaurants have been intentionally blocked by the enemy? Were there areas of our lives in which we were experiencing a detained answer to prayer or blessing? If there were, how often did I succumb to believing the enemy's lies about them?

I do not believe that every unanswered prayer or unfulfilled blessing is a result of the enemy's interference. When the Apostle Paul insisted on asking for a thorn to be removed from his side, the Lord told him, "My grace is all you need. My power works best in weakness" (2 Cor. 12:9). The Apostle Paul had a lesson to learn about his weakness, the Lord's grace, and the strength to be found in these. It was a lesson in developing his character, letting go of his self-reliance, and completely surrendering to God.

Still, Daniel's experience is relevant to understanding our own experiences with unanswered prayers or unfulfilled blessings. Although it does not apply to every situation, we should always take our Heavenly Father's intentions towards us into account. He desires to bless us in extraordinary and extravagant ways; that is our Father's heart. Recognizing this truth should open our eyes and allow us to break free from any distortions of that reality we may hold.

God promised abundant life to each and every one of us. I am not promoting prosperity theology here. Abundance in life is not purely financial. Abundance is holistic. We can experience abundance in our relationships, in our quality of life, and in our emotional health. The key is to become aware of areas where we may be experiencing lack, then effectively pray, according to our Heavenly Father's intentions, to partake in the fullness of His blessings for us.

Claiming What Is Rightfully Yours

Shortly after we established our first safe house for survivors of human trafficking, some of our close friends from the United States visited us. One of them shared an interesting tidbit of information that gave us deeper understanding about unanswered prayers and unfulfilled blessings. He showed us a prayer by a Satanist. The prayer asked demons to be empowered to steal answers to prayers and blessings from believers, and to deliver them to witches and Satanists instead. Think about that. Satanists are actively praying right now for demons to be strengthened to steal answers to prayers and blessings. That infuriates me. Meanwhile, Christians often beg God to hear their prayers, thinking the problem is that God isn't listening to them. Don't be fooled; this is a lie straight from hell. 1 John 5:14-15 reads:

> And we are confident that he hears us
> whenever we ask for anything that pleases
> him. And since we know he hears us when
> we make our requests, we also know that
> he will give us what we ask for.

We must be confident that God hears us and intends to give us what we ask for. I am not promoting "name and claim it" prayers where you petition for every selfish desire you have. I'm not saying we should all ask for millions of dollars to give us financial stability, even if we try to justify it by saying we will give half away. Whatever we ask for must be pleasing to the Lord. As an exercise, I encourage you to review the prayers that Jesus said throughout the Gospel narratives. Notice the common themes and use them as a model in your own prayer life to ensure that you are not deviating from what is pleasing to the Lord. If you pray the same types of prayers as Jesus', they will be pleasing to God.

Differently from "name and claim it" prayers, there are prayers that I call "taking back what is rightfully yours." Think for a moment about everything that God placed in you before you were born. You have innate characteristics of your personality, God's fingerprint on your life, which are unique to you as a person. Some people refer to this as your original design. In your lifetime, you may have experienced trauma or pain that significantly and negatively impacted your self-perception. The enemy often seizes the opportunity in those moments to steal your ability to live out the fullness of your original design by placing filters that distort your self-image and, ultimately, your view of God.

After being sexually abused, I personally struggled for years to believe that I could be sexually pure. My innocence was robbed, which warped my belief system, causing me to believe I could no longer be pure. I was operating out of guilt and shame. In truth, innocence and purity are a part of my original design. To restore them, I had to take steps in prayer and rescue back everything that my painful experience stole from me. I realized that I was falling short of my potential because I had not proactively claimed what was rightfully mine, which is everything God placed in me before I was even born. Realizing this was like noticing that a robber had stolen something right out of my hands, and I could finally take back what belongs to me because Jesus legally restored it to me on the cross. I wanted to fight my way through prayer to reclaim everything that had been stolen, lost, or distorted, and to restore all that God had originally placed in me. It was like finding all the missing pieces to a puzzle, putting them together, and showing off a masterpiece that God had always intended the world to see.

I had to replace my perception of reality based on circumstances with a view of reality firmly based on God's promises. It's in this mindset shift that a lot of people lose the battle. When I did it, it felt like rediscovering God. I had to relearn all of His promises and intentions for me. Truth had to prevail over all the disappointments and sinful struggles of my life. This changed my hazy perception of God to a clear image of His loving character.

I started to pray like this for all the blessings I knew I was missing out on. Like answers to prayers, blessings flow out of God's throne into our lives. These blessings are not petitioned for out of selfish ambition. Our loving Heavenly Father desires to pour these blessings on us simply because we are His children. It's the same principle as reclaiming what is part of our original design. Think of it like this: Someone who loves you promised you a gift. It's intended for you to receive, but someone else wants to meddle in the

Painful Miracles

delivery process. Don't you want to make sure that you receive your gift? The gift is a blessing from God, and you are the sole recipient.

When we begin the process of praying to reclaim what has been stolen from us or distorted, there are key principles to keep in mind. First, knowing who we are in Christ primes us for effective prayer. This may seem obvious, but let me frame it another helpful way: For most of my Christian life, I sought God's approval by trying to show that I was "being a good son." This presupposes that I can attain "goodness" through proper behavior or acts of compassion, which is performance-based acceptance that is out of alignment with the Gospel. Now I know that my main focus should be on "being good at being a son." My identity as God's son is the focus, and my efforts are based on it. The goal is to see how good I can be at being a son. To get here, I had to renounce all my attempts at performance-based acceptance and fully embrace my identity.

Second, it's critical that we surrender all our pain and the distortions that we incurred as a result of loss. You may have forgiven people who damaged you, but have you surrendered to God all the pain that you experienced? Doing so releases the enemy's foothold that could spawn resentment in your heart. I had to list on paper all of the negative impacts and feelings I had and surrender them to God one by one in prayer. I prayed these prayers out loud, which I encourage you to do. Make a vocal proclamation surrendering your pain to God so that you and the enemy can hear it. After this, I asked for a blessing to fill the space of everything that was surrendered. For instance, I surrendered neglect and asked for belonging and acceptance to replace it. If you surrender depression, ask for never-ceasing joy. Whatever was in the place of brokenness, take steps to fill it with wholeness.

When we pray to claim what is rightfully ours in Christ, we should directly contrast the prayers of a Satanist: "I pray that angels will be strengthened by God's power to deliver blessings and answers to prayers. I pray that these will be delivered on time. I also pray that the blessings and answers will be lacking in nothing, that they will be in complete accordance to how God intended them when He spoke them from His throne." Think about delivery systems for a moment. When we order things online, we expect our orders to be delivered on time, to be undamaged and not missing any parts. We should expect the same every time we pray.

Continuing the prayer: "I also proclaim my spiritual rights. I have authority to do so because I am the legal recipient of those blessings and answers by the blood of Christ. I rebuke the enemy's attempts to alter or rob them from me." When you know you have certain rights, don't you make sure to protect them? Similarly, we should claim what is rightfully ours in Christ.

Chapter 6: Men in White

Letters from a Hitman

I vividly remember receiving a frantic phone call from our transition home director one early morning. She was alarmed by a handwritten letter that someone had just slid under the door. The letter was from a *sicario*, which means hitman in Spanish, and was directed to one of our beneficiaries, whom we'll call Karla.

Karla was hiding from the cartel, who had trafficked her all over Mexico. We were providing witness protection for Karla while she testified to the federal police, supplying intel on a case against the cartel. The letter included death threats against her and us for giving the police information on the cartel. They gave Karla one week to leave the city or they would kill her and us.

Our director was frightened, but I calmly told her to have all the beneficiaries at the transition home pack up their belongings as fast as they could, because I was going to pick them up. While they were packing, the director saw another letter slide under the door. It was a second letter from the *sicario* telling Karla she now had until the end of the day to leave the city.

I had an exit plan. The girls would leave the transition home in one car and, at a pre-established rendezvous point, I would pick them up and take them to our home. I also arranged for a staff member to meet us at the rendezvous point and take Karla out of the city, where she would be safer.

Upon meeting at the rendezvous point, Karla apologized continuously for bringing us so much trouble, but I reassured her everything would be alright. I then took our transition home director and the rest of our beneficiaries to our home. Nervous and frightened, they all settled in.

There was something unusual about the handwritten letters from the *sicario*. Aside from the awkward lettering and numerous spelling mistakes, he made some surprising statements on top of the death threats. Firstly, he said Karla was a liar because she told him that her father had passed away years ago. Karla reassured us her father did pass away and she didn't understand why he was mentioning that in the letter. The letter said, "You're a liar, because you said your father died, but I am constantly being visited by two men in white who say they've been sent by your father."

When Karla arrived at our transition home five years ago, she was scared and disheveled from her experiences as a victim of sex trafficking. Although she tried to maintain her resolve in giving her testimony to the federal police, she constantly sought peace for her soul through prayers that we offered her. It wasn't long before Karla decided to give her life to Jesus. The two men dressed in white sent by Karla's father? The only explanation is that they were angels, and the father who had sent them was Karla's Heavenly Father.

The second unusual aspect of the *sicario's* letters is he wrote that he knew Karla had become a powerful woman. There was almost a tone of awe and fear in the letter. It was surprising that he spoke of Karla's power while threatening to kill her, but it was another confirmation of Karla's genuine faith. It reassured me of the position of true authority and power we have as God's sons and daughters.

Lastly, the *sicario* mentioned that the two men dressed in white told him to leave Karla alone and spoke to him about Jesus' forgiveness. What an amazing expression of the persistent love of our Heavenly Father who extends His forgiveness to even the worst criminals. God's grace goes beyond our human ability to forgive.

We took the *sicario's* handwritten letters to the federal police. They did fingerprint testing and a handwriting analysis. They verified the letters were authentic, but the content perplexed them. We took the opportunity to share who we believed the two men in white were and about Jesus' forgiveness. It was a unique opportunity to share a testimony with federal officials.

The director and other beneficiaries were at our home for about a month when the director approached me to say she believed the time had come for them to go back to their house. Still concerned about the threat to their security, we had been planning on finding a house in a different location for them. However, the director firmly said she didn't want to fear men above God and she knew God was going to protect them. What an incredible statement of great faith! They went home, and we felt overwhelming peace about our decision. No more security issues happened after that incident. Karla made monthly visits to the city, and we continued to assist her until she finished making her statements to the federal police.

An Unseen Army

In 2 Kings 6, the prophet Elisha was wanted for capture by his king's enemy. Surrounded at night by horses and chariots, Elisha's servant was overwhelmed with fear of the enemy's encroaching army. Elisha prayed to the Lord, asking that his servant's eyes be opened to see what he saw. When the servant opened his eyes, he saw that horses and chariots of fire filled the hills all around them. He was able to see God's unseen army, sent to guarantee their protection and victory. We witnessed something similar when two men dressed in white were sent to protect us from a dangerous person threatening to kill us.

I am now even more confident that God protects me, my family, and my staff. My confidence does not come from what I can visibly see, but from God's promise about His presence. I know with certainty that if I am in His presence, I will also have His divine protection.

When we first started our ministry, we knew the risks we were taking. Fighting human trafficking in Mexico means confronting violent cartels and criminals. I could potentially lose my life, since seeking to dismantle a significant revenue stream for the cartel can lead to their fighting back at any moment. We knew the risks involved with this type of ministry, but we could not ignore God's call in our lives.

Throughout the years, many people have asked me about the risks involved in our work. They ask if I am scared for the safety of my family or if any threats were made against us. My answer is always, "Yes, we've faced multiple death threats, and we take the necessary safety precautions, but threats made by men are no challenge for God's justice."

I can't think about our ministry in terms of risks versus rewards. I had to abandon ideas of trying to make sense of everything. My choices have to be out of obedience. My obedience consists of staying strong in my commitment to see God's justice on the earth, no matter what obstacles or dangers are before me. Obedience means being confident in the knowledge that God called me, I answered, and He will be faithful to complete the work.

Do You Trust Me?

One of the most classic scenes from the 1992 Disney animation movie *Aladdin* is when Princess Jasmine suspects that Prince Ali could be Aladdin, the "street rat" she met on the streets of the fictional city Agrabah while she was running away from the palace and an arranged marriage. Aladdin helped Jasmine find a hiding place with a beautiful view of the palace. When the palace guards suddenly appeared and there was nowhere to run, Aladdin reached out his hand to the Princess and asked, "Do you trust me?" They leapt out the window to escape the guards.

Fast forward to the scene in which Aladdin is posing as Prince Ali, talking to Princess Jasmine in her chambers on a beautiful Arabian evening with clear skies. Trying to escape an awkward conversation, Prince Ali/Aladdin steps off the palace balcony onto a magic carpet. He reaches out his hand to Princess Jasmine and asks a familiar question, "Do you trust me?" Jasmine responds curiously, "What?" Again, he asks, "Do you trust me?" This strangely familiar question is how Princess Jasmine begins to suspect that Prince Ali is actually Aladdin in disguise.

I believe that God is constantly asking us the same question that Aladdin asked Princess Jasmine: "Do you trust me?" This question challenges us in our faith to put all of our trust in God and forfeit our trust in everything else that has kept us stable. Trusting God can take us out of our comfort zone and into unfamiliar places, but He is present in these places. God's promise to be present with us gives us courage to go anywhere and do anything for His kingdom.

I Found Myself Under a Table

When I was in college at George Mason University in Northern Virginia, my friends were going to drive up to Philadelphia for a retreat to learn about missions. I decided to go along because I wanted to hang out with them, even though I wasn't very interested in missions. On our last night, there was a time of prayer. The lights were dimmed and a keyboard played softly in the background as one of the pastors led us in prayer. I don't remember how or why, but I found myself on my knees under a table, holding on to its legs with both of my hands. It was as if I didn't want to let go of something. Then, I heard a clear, soft voice ask, "Do you trust me?" I knew it was God. Again, He asked, "Do you trust me?" I started complaining to Him because I felt like the question was unfair. God knew that I couldn't say no, but I knew the consequences of saying yes. Although I was initially hesitant, when I finally said yes, a flood of joy and high expectations released. Everything in my life up to that point made more sense. Then, I heard the clear, soft voice say, "Now go."

I gave my life for missions that night despite my initial disinterest. Most of my negativity about missions came from my own experiences as a child of missionary parents. Before the retreat, I knew I wanted to serve God with my life, but I wanted to do anything except become a missionary. It wasn't that my experience growing up overseas was bad. Some of my fondest memories are from our time as a family in South America. Our experiences there shaped me and positively impacted my personal development. I learned a third language and gained an understanding of different cultures.

My main concern with committing my life to missions was financial. I saw my parents struggle financially both on the mission field and coming back from it. We never had to skip meals, but when I returned to the United States for college, I noticed a significant difference between the financial situation of my childhood friends' families and of my family. My father had a difficult time finding another job and making ends meet after missions. It was hard for me to watch him struggle. It saddened me deeply.

I didn't want to become a missionary because I had established a standard for myself to have the financial freedom to buy my children whatever they wanted for Christmas. However, God wanted me to surrender my standard and all discomfort stemming from painful past experiences in missions. None of these conditions or experiences were for me to carry; they were burdens that held me back from God's purpose for my future.

It's a challenge to identify what's holding us back and dig into our past to see where it comes from. You may be currently held back by the same thing that held me back: deep discomfort or pain from past experiences. We must clearly discern what emotions we have or commitments we made in response to these memories. Once we identify all of those pieces, we must submit them to the Lordship of God. Surrendering these is not easy. You may have created an entire worldview based on your past experiences, but God wants to be the Lord of your entire life. When Jesus carried all of our sins with Him to the cross, He also carried all the burdens and pain that sin caused in our lives.

I encourage you to take a moment to identify what may be holding you back from your God-given purpose. Dive deep into your past. I pray that as you do this, the Holy Spirit will guide you, comfort you, and heal your past wounds. Once you identify all the pieces holding you back, make sure to say out loud that you are surrendering those burdens to God and invite His Lordship into those areas of your life.

Favored Protection

Many of us regularly say a prayer of protection over ourselves, our family, and our loved ones. It becomes a part of our prayer routine to ask that God protect us from harm or any opposition that may come our way. What I learned from the experience with the "men dressed in white" is that divine protection is constantly available to us when we are advancing God's Kingdom. This is what I call "favored protection."

When you are advancing God's Kingdom, God knows that you will face opposition on many levels and He provides

His favored protection when you confront them. This is because there is inherent risk and danger involved when overtaking enemy territory. Although enemy retaliation is inevitable, God's purposes will always be fulfilled. Consequently, favored protection gets you *through* the enemy's attacks, but it won't keep you away *from* them. It will get you *through* the storm, but it won't get you a way *around* it.

Many of you want to live a life of radical faith, but you're concerned with financial stability, uncertain about the future, and filled with self-doubt. I encourage you to trust God and be fully confident that He will protect you and your family as you take bold steps of faith. He will provide for your every need as you advance His Kingdom. He reminds you that the most important part of your identity is knowing that you are His child. God is holding His hand out to you asking you to trust Him. All you have to do is take His hand and say, "Yes."

Chapter 7: Walk; Don't Run

Summertime

When I was a child, I spent lots of time at the community pool in the summer. I have fond memories of keeping my eyes open under water until they were red and burning, hearing 80's pop music blast through the pool's speaker system, playing "Sharks and Minnows" and "Marco Polo," and regularly getting in trouble with lifeguards.

When the other kids and I got out of the water to play games or for mandatory swim breaks, we'd hear lifeguards blow their whistles at us and shout, "Walk! Don't run!" In a child's mind, that's impossible. How was I supposed to walk when I needed to win a game or run away from a little girl my friends and I were teasing? I know the lifeguards' warnings were well intended, but they felt like exaggerated requests to us. As a compromise, many of us "walk-ran," which is awkward speed-walking with stiff arms and legs. You move faster than when you walk, but slightly slower than when you run. Of course, when the lifeguards weren't looking, we just ran.

I applied this same hurried pace to my life as I got older. I've always been eager to get to places quickly. When I started working, I wanted to achieve a lot in ministry by maintaining an accelerated rhythm. I believed the more I could accomplish in a short amount of time, the more successful I was. This is also partly due to my competitive nature. For better or worse, I've always preferred to see everyone else in my rear-view mirror than see their taillights ahead of me.

When it comes to ministry, I believed that I was justified in my reasoning. We are fighting against human trafficking, and traffickers stay awake all night scheming. I told myself I had to at least match their intensity. I believe we can bring an end to modern-day slavery and human trafficking by the next generation. Even if we can't achieve total global eradication of slavery, we can take significant strides towards that end. For that to happen, a lot must be done in limited time, which is why I worked tirelessly to ensure that we made meaningful progress.

Many people can relate to working unrelentingly towards a goal, whether the goal is getting in physical shape or doing something for the greater good of humanity. Regardless, the visions we have of the future can consume us. Either the end seems so unattainable that we lose hope and give up, or we are so intense in our approach that we lose all our energy in trying to sustain an unrealistic pace.

The latter is called burning out, and it's happened to me. I felt like a kid at the community pool again, trying to run as often and hard as possible. It was almost intoxicating, but as time passed, I demanded more and more of myself and my team until it was too much.

Assuming an Unhealthy Number of Responsibilities

We started our anti-trafficking work with one project: an aftercare facility. One safe house was a lot of work, as it required an immense amount of attention and energy. Still, it was always our vision to expand to different areas of fighting against human trafficking, because we knew we needed a holistic approach to see real transformation in the city and country.

We prioritized prevention and intervention programs. We started running block parties, showing virtual reality videos in schools and at public events, and we opened a community center in the red-light district. Then, we created a new restoration program: a jewelry brand that employs women who decide to leave their lives in prostitution. Lastly, we opened a transition home for girls who age out of our safe house program. We were growing quickly, and our work load was increasing significantly.

To run these new projects, we needed more staff members and volunteers. It felt like, overnight, we were suddenly managing three times as many people than usual. Everyone was passionate about their work, which was an enormous blessing and made up for my blunders as a leader. I was comfortable leading a small group, but leading an organization was extremely challenging.

With this expansion, our annual budget grew exponentially. At the time, the burden of fundraising fell solely on my shoulders. This caused an unusual amount of mental and emotional stress in me. It didn't help that I often said to our team, "Don't worry about money. I will take care of finances; just focus on your work with the beneficiaries." I was fooling myself assuming I could do that, since I didn't have the slightest clue how to fundraise properly for a nonprofit organization. I relied heavily on individuals and churches to donate. Writing grants and working closely with larger foundations were completely foreign concepts to me, which limited my ability to raise large sums of money, a necessary part of sustaining the growth of an organization.

However, the problems we faced from growing too quickly as an organization didn't compare to the problems I personally faced in assuming too much individual responsibility for our ministry's success. I bottled up a lot of anxiety and stress that accumulated from managing our team and fundraising. A fearful voice inside me repeated, "You're not going to be able to raise the money you need for next month. What are you going to do?" The voice held more power over me than years of memories of God's faithfulness and provision. Deep down, I knew God had everything under control, but my anxiety monopolized my attention to the point I couldn't focus on positioning myself to fully depend on God. My stress drove me to work more, and I falsely assumed that I could cure my anxiety by staying busy or producing results. I was stuck in an unending vicious cycle.

A Rock Spoke to Me

During this tumultuous season of stress and anxiety, I had an opportunity to get away and go to a conference in the United States. I belonged to an international cohort of leaders who were doing phenomenal social justice work around the world. Our cohort leader arranged for those of us who were fighting against human trafficking to meet at a Christian conference about prostitution. Four of us from this special cohort attended, along with a couple hundred more people.

Painful Miracles

I had time to disconnect from the weight of my responsibilities and decompress. Even the drive to the conference center was relaxing. It was a clear day, and my skin tingled from all the beautiful, green trees I saw.

During the conference, I paid particularly close attention to the other members of my cohort. They were all seasoned professionals, well-accomplished and respected by their peers. Some of them were accompanied by a supporting staff member who traveled thousands of miles to help them with their presentations and stay updated on what was happening in their organizations. Meanwhile, I was clueless as to what was happening at my nonprofit in Mexico, and I felt out of my league compared to them.

Late one afternoon, the four of us decided to escape the conference for a moment to share our stories with each other around a table. As the other three spoke, they shared similar struggles as mine. Even though they were at different stages as leaders of their organizations, we all shared similar success stories and hardships. It was life-giving for me, because I realized I was not alone in my leadership challenges. I got new, greater perspective on the health and growth of our ministry in Mexico. I confessed that I was foolishly carrying burdens that did not belong to me. I cherish the afternoon I shared with those three leaders, with whom I found profound camaraderie, a kinship that exists to this day.

Everyone at the conference was required to participate in the last group activity. While we all gathered in the main auditorium, facilitators approached us, showed us a table covered in rocks, and explained that a prayer team had written inspirational messages on them earlier that day. They instructed us to pray and ask God to speak to us. Then, we were supposed to go to the table and choose a rock with the message meant for us.

I listened intently to the instructions while sitting on the floor in the back of the auditorium. I thought to myself, "I need to receive a good word before leaving this place." As other people made their way forward, I leaned my back against the wall behind me, positioned my face toward Heaven, and began to pray. After a short while, I slowly made my way to the table. It was filled with scattered rocks that varied in color. The words written on them were faced down. My hand hovered over the rocks until I chose a rugged white one, which I knew was the right one for me. I held on tightly to the rock in my hand and walked back to my seat on the floor in the back of the auditorium. I closed my eyes one more time before opening my hand to read what was written on the rock. It read, "Walk slow."

I started sobbing all by myself while a weight as heavy as a mountain fell off my shoulders. All of the stress and anxiety that had built up over years started to dissipate while I meditated on the two words that were a healing balm for my soul.

Walk Slow and Walk Well

The message was, "Walk slow." Walking slowly was a foreign concept to me. I had always been in a hurry to accomplish and achieve things, so I never really considered walking slowly as an option. I often criticized people who walked slowly, since I saw walking as means to a destination.

The destination was always more important to me than the process of getting there.

That day, I saw the danger in that approach to building an organization or ministry. You can become consumed with the destination and disregard the overall health of your team. Historically, people and leaders of movements who justified the means by the end found themselves in a great deal of trouble. That was not the path I wanted to be on, so I had to learn to walk slower.

I had to let go of the frenetic pace I was operating at and surrender the value I placed on achievements. It was like taking my foot off the gas pedal of my car. Just like some of us enjoy the thrill of driving fast or getting to our destination as quickly as possible, I was enjoying the thrill of moving our ministry to grow quickly. However, our achievements caused detriment to my personal health and the organization's health. My selfish ambition was in the driver's seat, and I had to take back control.

When you realize you're driving a vehicle too quickly, the police may stop you and give you a speeding ticket, you may get into an accident, or the engine may fail from being pushed too hard. There are warning signs that let you know you should slow down, but are you willing to pay attention to them and actually slow down? Walking slowly meant taking the risk of exposing myself to myself and my team, then deprioritizing my goals and giving preference to my emotional well-being and the emotional well-being of others. Walking slowly also meant surrendering the value I placed on achieving results, which I'll discuss in more detail in the next chapter.

We eventually incorporated "walk slow" into our organization's culture statements and added "walk well" to it. Slowing down isn't enough. Rest is crucial, but if we jump back into the same rushed rhythm after resting, then we miss the point. Walking well is leading a healthy life. It's prioritizing the important things above the urgent. Walking well means that you value relationships over tasks.

Leaders emphasize vision. We esteem leaders or organizations that have great vision. Vision is important, but how you get to your vision is equally as important. The process for achieving a vision must be a priority. Developing character and integrity is crucial; they are just as important as the base of a building is to the building itself. A building without a base may seem impressive, but it's bound to collapse after a couple challenges. Jesus mentions the value of character in chapter seven of the book of Matthew, comparing it to building a house on solid rock as opposed to sand.

In addition to prioritizing the process of achieving a vision and developing character and integrity, in walking well, congruency is crucial. Congruency involves integrity, but with a clear practical application. Walking well means being congruent in what you say and do. It means that whatever you think or feel is congruent with how you express yourself. Walking well means that your private, unseen life is congruent with your public life.

A Joyous Rhythm

For some people, the mere thought of walking slowly is frightening, but they can find joy in it. Joy is more than an emotion. It's an antidote to stress and anxiety. Joy helps bring frustrations into perspective and can be a shield for our souls. Being joyful in everything we do is crucial to our ability to walk slowly and well. I have learned three key lessons about being joyful while walking slowly.

The first lesson I learned at a conference during a dark period of my life. This darkness had nothing to do with the pressures of leadership, but with the darkness involved in fighting human trafficking in general. In this ministry, we routinely confront demonic possessions, satanic curses, and witchcraft. At the time of the conference, I had absorbed lots of evil and provided the enemy with a foothold to influence me. As a result, I had made an inner vow accepting personal responsibility for our beneficiaries' deliverance from evil.

The conference's main speaker read Philippians 4:4, which says, "Always be full of joy in the Lord, I say it again - rejoice!" In no other instance in the Bible is a commandment repeated successively in this way. The immediate reiteration of it demonstrates this commandment's importance and how vital it is that we obey it. I allowed joy to become completely absent from my life. Instantly after hearing that verse spoken, I was a messy blob of tears and snot repenting for my lack of joy. I understood that being joyful is a commandment and that I was living in disobedience. Being full of joy became an act of obedience, not an emotive state. I knew I had to decide to no longer invite darkness into my life but make a conscious effort to always walk towards the light.

The second lesson I learned is to become increasingly aware of God's presence, where there is constant and eternal joy. God is the most joyful being in the universe. When you are in the Lord's presence, joy is absolutely inevitable. Why not make every effort to be consistently in His presence then? Practically, I try to make worship a priority in my day. That typically includes listening to worship music in the morning, having instrumental worship play as I meditate on God's word, and playing worship music myself with instruments. Taking it a step further, we should realize that everything we do can be worship unto the Lord. Our job, chores, and even parenting can be intentional worship to God. The key is consecration.

Consecrate your day and all of its activities to the Lord every morning or at every chance you get. Consecrate yourself through prayer to be presented as a living sacrifice. Here is an example of a prayer you can say, adapted from Pastor Ed Salas:

> I come in the name, power, and authority of the Lord Jesus Christ of Nazareth to present my body and all that I am as a living sacrifice to be used for Your glory, God. I pray for Christ's blood to sanctify my body, mind, and emotions as I dedicate myself fully to You. I pray for Your holy fire to burn away every impurity in me. Holy Spirit, fill me and help me live under the complete Lordship of Jesus. I present my body as a temple for the Holy Spirit, for Your glory and power. I desire and dedicate myself to You so Your glory and power may flow through me. In the name of Jesus Christ, I pray. Amen.

In the Bible, worship and consecration precede breakthrough and victory. Worship is our preparation. Being prepared for our daily challenges does not come from our training, knowledge, or capacity. In the Scriptures, we see that God did not always choose the capable. He chose those with a broken and contrite spirit. Our consecration and worship to the Lord position our hearts with humility. As we prepare ourselves through consecration, we experience the fullness of God's presence. In His presence, there is constant joy.

The last lesson I learned is that joy comes from knowing that God's mercy is much greater than our own. On many occasions, I have prayed for God's breakthrough in my life or someone else's. Sometimes, I got frustrated from not seeing the results I expected, and I questioned God's mercy. I've learned not to question it anymore, because I know now that His mercy is preeminent, extravagant, and certainly greater than what I can perceive with my puny human mind. There is enormous solace and peace in this knowledge, the type of divine peace that precedes joy.

If you have ever challenged God's mercy, I encourage you to take a moment and confess that. Then, declare God's holy mercy abounding in your life, in accordance to His perfect will. I guarantee that joy will fill your soul.

Chapter 8: Stop Worrying about the Results

Nothing to Prove

At the time of writing this book, my wife and I have been married for over 21 years. After all these years, we still feel passion and deep love for each other. We hardly argue anymore. I can probably count on one hand how many times we've argued in the past couple of years. It hasn't always been this way, though. In the first years of our marriage, we argued and disagreed a lot. Since then, we have discovered keys to peace in our home and marriage.

The first key is something we refer to as a spiritual cleansing prayer. We routinely say a spiritual cleansing prayer after returning from certain places in Mexico City, especially the red-light districts, or after interacting with people carrying a lot of darkness or heaviness. These prayers help us keep negativity and demonic influences out of our marriage and home.

I remember returning from our community center in the red-light district one afternoon and telling my family crass jokes. My wife turned to me and asked, "Did you say a cleansing prayer?" It had totally slipped my mind, so I promptly prayed, cleansing myself of any vulgar influences, and blessed my mind and mouth with purity. After the prayer, the urge to say anything out of line instantly dissipated. Through experiences like this one, my family learned not to immediately associate someone's behavior with who they are as a person.

The second epiphany came after we had been married for seven years. We still argued a lot, and I was getting tired of fighting. I knew we could have a better marriage. I started paying attention to the details of our arguments: what was said, how I felt, how we both reacted, and how the disagreement escalated. After an in-depth play-by-play, I realized that most, if not all of our arguments, stemmed from my desire to be seen and known as a good husband and father.

Most people want to be seen and heard to some degree. We want to maintain a positive image in social situations, including at work, at church, and at home. This is especially true in the social media world. We carefully update our social media profiles with the best parts of our days and prune away anything that causes consternation. Some of us get obsessed with how our profiles and posts compare to others'. We get stuck in an endless comparison game. At the end of the day, what are we really trying to prove to ourselves or to other people? Do we want people to think more highly of us according to what we post? What if we had nothing to prove?

I realized the reason for the vast majority of my arguments with my wife was my inability to be what I perceived was a good husband or father. If anything said or done challenged my image as either of those, I fought to defend myself. For example, after a long day at work, I often came home feeling tired and forgot to do something as inconsequential as taking out the trash. My wife would ask me if I had taken out the trash, and I would feel offended and start arguing with her. I would tell her I had a long, tiring day at work and she shouldn't think that I was a lazy person. I would explain that I was working hard at being a provider for my family and shouldn't be judged for something as meaningless as taking out the trash. This exaggerated example shows how even something small felt threatening to my image of myself. Sometimes our arguments happened over days or months. At the end of the day, the problem was always that what was said offended the image I was trying to preserve.

I also realized that I connected this image of myself directly to how worthy I felt to receive love. In other words, faults and cracks in my image made me feel unworthy to receive love. That's why I fought so hard to maintain my image. Obviously, my worth and the love I receive are not connected to my image of myself. My wife loves me and accepts me for who I am. I don't need to prove my worth in order to receive love or acceptance, because all of the love and acceptance I could want or need have already been given to me.

Many of us are conditioned as children to think the way I did. My parents were happy with me when I got good grades at school and were upset with me when I didn't. It was hard to understand that no matter how good or bad my grades were, my parents' love for me never changed. We are easily sucked into directly correlating our performance with being accepted. If we understood that we are already loved and accepted, what would change for us?

When I stopped worrying about keeping up my image as a good father and husband, a heavy burden came off my shoulders. The change didn't happen overnight; the process of learning to live according to the truth was gradual. Just like we can develop muscular atrophy after an injury, we can also develop emotional atrophy from lies that distort our self-image. I had to constantly repeat to myself that I was loved just as I was. Eventually, the reasons I had for fighting and arguing with my wife felt petty and non-sensical. I put more effort into building something beautiful rather than trying to prove that I was good enough to be loved according to false expectations for myself.

Another personal breakthrough happened when I was able to take the concept of "nothing to prove" to our ministry. What if I didn't have to prove anything at work or in my service to God? What if the only affirmation I needed to rely upon or base my life on was the simple truth that God loves me? Success and achievements would be byproducts of an intimate relationship with God rather than the purpose of it. The goal of building a big and successful ministry would lose its hype and glamor. The focus would no longer be on what I can attain, but who I can become.

Called to Love People, Not Change People

We are called to love people as God loves them. We are not called to change people; that's not our job. It's the Holy Spirit's job to bring conviction where it's needed, and He doesn't need us to convict people of their sins. The Holy Spirit sanctifies us to make us more like Jesus, but it's not our responsibility to transform people to be who we want them to be. When we try to do God's job in someone's life, it's unlikely to turn out well. I don't know about you, but I certainly don't want to stand in God's way.

Many of us have mistakenly spent an enormous amount of misdirected energy trying to catalyze change in people. We do this when we want to see someone we love, like a family member or friend, escape struggles such as addiction or depression. We see them struggle and feel a sincere desire to see them in a better place, but we should not confuse our earnest wishes with God's will for their lives. If we were to place our earnest wishes and God's transformative power on a scale to see what benefits people more, the two don't even compare. What if we invested more of our energy into loving people so that they experience the Father's embrace?

Sometimes we attempt to catalyze change for an organization, our church, or our community, anywhere we want to see social changes. These endeavors are based on a protagonist mindset. The danger here is subtle, but made evident by our perceptions and beliefs. In short, our pitfall is pride. When we look at certain problems in an organization or society, we may have ideas to improve things. That can be helpful, but problems emerge when we think we "know better."

"Knowing better" and making things better are different. "Knowing better" is thinking that your ideas, perceptions, and beliefs are superior to those of others in the room. It sometimes even involves insisting that your ideas be moved forward and exhibiting dominant behavior. We are not called to impose our ideas and dominate others. We are called to serve. We are called to follow Jesus' example and wash other people's feet.

Making things better means being willing to serve people humbly and sacrificially. From that position, with a towel wrapped around our waist and soap and water in our hands, we are able to sit down with others and come up with solutions to problems. The key word here is "with." What we should avoid is attempting to develop solutions *for* others. Working *with* others implies involving our community and being willing to work out differences for a common goal. This path is not faster, but it's much better. When done right, it's also more sustainable.

Stop Worrying about the Results

For many years, I spent an enormous amount of emotional energy seeking results to validate my value as a leader. When I learned that I really didn't have anything to prove and that true transformation is in God's hands, I stopped being driven by results. Results are not my responsibility; they are God's responsibility. Loving people well, being good at being God's child, and being disciplined in developing Christ-like character are my responsibilities. My focus is firmly placed on these efforts, and it's clear to me I shouldn't worry about my results. Getting to this point isn't like turning off a light switch. For me, it involved a process and key lessons that I will now share.

Worrying comes in different shapes and colors. The type of worrying I refer to here is not the type that is full of anxiety. It's worry that looks like deep concern, but doesn't consume your every waking hour. In essence, it may even seem positive, as though it's "responsible worry". However, it's not what we are called to do. As our ministry grew, I worried that we were not raising enough funds to meet our projected budget. We were diligent in finding and keeping donors, we stewarded our resources prudently, we weren't haphazard in our fundraising approach, and we didn't spend money carelessly. Despite all this, we often only had one month's worth of funding in our bank account. It seemed like a perfect time to justify worrying about results, which in this case were the donations we could raise in any given month.

Instead, we consciously decided not to worry about our finances. We placed all our confidence in God's faithfulness to provide divinely and focused our energies on our work rescuing and restoring victims of human trafficking. These were conscious and proactive decisions we had to make. We knew if we did our part in trusting God, He would show us His faithfulness. Today, we can testify that after over ten years, even with financial ups and downs, we have never missed a single payroll or failed to pay any of our bills on time.

There is an insidious side to being obsessed with results. Our competitiveness can cause us to blindly obsess over results and equate exceptional results with success. We deviously justify our drive for success by saying the work and results glorify God, yet God never called us to success in this way. I believe He is more pleased when we serve in a way that contributes to other people's success. Imagine if we measured our success by the success of others around us. I believe we could quench competitiveness by focusing our energies in lifting up our fellow brothers and sisters in Christ, rather than focusing on our personal achievements and accolades. That doesn't mean successful Christians or ministries won't exist. On the contrary, I believe God extravagantly blesses those who are faithful and contrite in spirit, but it matters how we achieve goals and how we position our hearts along the way.

There is another reason we must be careful with obsessing over results: Results, measurable data of an activity's outcome, don't always equate to transformation. For instance, results can be the number of people who attended an event or the number of views of an online post. We cannot be enamored with these numbers and assume that we are making a significant impact, because that's not always the case. Many leaders lose their direction by touting their results as real change.

Sustainable and lasting change doesn't only come from high attendance rates at conferences. We shouldn't discount the value of these results, and we should measure them, but we also need to take deliberate steps to move forward from the results-oriented stage of short-term influence toward the affect stage of change that then leads to long-term impact.

The affect stage is when people's behaviors, attitudes, or knowledge change due to measurable experiences in the results stage. For example, let's pretend you are running a community hygiene campaign. As part of the campaign, you teach people how to wash their hands properly. The results are the number of people you taught to wash their hands. The affect stage happens when people effectively wash their hands on their own. You know you've reached this stage when, after some time, you return to the community and observe that hand washing has been integrated into people's daily routines. You can also interview people in the community, asking how they feel about this new habit and whether they feel that washing their hands is contributing to stopping communicable diseases.

The impact stage is long-term, where sustainable and lasting transformation is established. Impact requires a transition from individual change to community change. This can be observed through a change in condition within the community. After the hand-washing campaign, for example, you could measure the number of times communicable diseases are contracted in the community and how much people's personal hygiene improved over a couple of years. Then, you could deduce whether overall health conditions in the community were impacted.

Using a logical framework to understand change dynamics is critical for leaders who desire to see transformation in their communities. It may seem overwhelming to attempt a long-term approach, but it's good stewardship of the knowledge and resources we have. Ultimately, transformation is in God's hands. Kingdoms are built with authority, infrastructure, and systems. As leaders, we have committed to seeing God's Kingdom established on earth as it is in Heaven. Therefore, we need to commit to building infrastructure and systems for God's Kingdom to flourish. If we already successfully built ministries and churches, we must now build the infrastructure needed for lasting transformation in our societies.

There is Only One Rescuer

To see change in the lives of loved ones, remember that there is only one Rescuer and His name is Jesus. Problems start when we attempt to rescue others ourselves, despite our good intentions of getting people out of harmful or difficult situations. There is nothing wrong with acts of grace, mercy, and kindness, but we must be careful not to take on the role of the rescuer.

Taking on the rescuer role inserts us into a drama triangle. In a drama triangle, there are three roles: the victim, the abuser, and the rescuer. The abuser causes the victim harm, and the victim seeks out a rescuer to free them from the abuser's hold. In a drama triangle, the victim often puts emotional pressure on the rescuer to do unreasonable things, manipulating them. Because of this, roles can be switched; the rescuer can suddenly become a victim and the victim an abuser. Many of us have experienced this when trying to help someone who manipulates us by guilting us into thinking we are solely responsible for their well-being. They may spit out accusations or engage in destructive behavior to get more of our attention. It is almost like getting caught in someone's emotional snare.

Some people don't have to be manipulated; they assume responsibility for others on their own. In both cases, the rescuer subjects themselves to a drama triangle, and the role switching continues until they remove themselves from the drama triangle.

The key principle I learned from helping people throughout the years is to constantly remind myself that there is only one rescuer. I must continually prayerfully

Painful Miracles

surrender the people I help to the Rescuer, Jesus, and point them to Him as much as I can. I also developed discernment and can quickly identify when someone is trying to manipulate me and suck me into a drama triangle. Red flags are phrases like, "You are never there for me" or, "You don't really care about me." The challenge is to be diligent in your discernment but steadfast in your compassion and mercy. Your heart cannot become hardened to the needs of others. I have seen people be cynical upon hearing of someone else's plight. Your heart must remain soft and your head sharp.

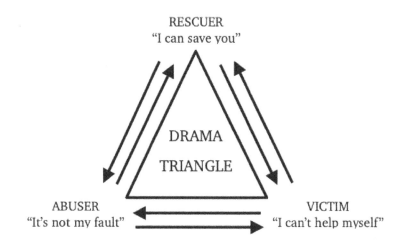

If you have felt other people's burdens and you have fallen into one or more drama triangles, I encourage you to take a moment and surrender these people and their predicaments to God. Release all of the emotional burdens that you're carrying. Proclaim that Jesus is the Rescuer and you are not. Pray that you will have the wisdom to serve these people, so that they will see Jesus as their only Rescuer. Pray that you will persevere in your Christ-like compassion towards the broken and lost. Commit to watching out for red flags while maintaining a tender heart in your next interactions.

Lastly, as we reflect on being called to love and not change people, I challenge you with this question: Do you believe God's love can transform people? If your answer is yes, then I encourage you not to be consumed by people's processes. If you are completely confident in the power of God's love to transform hearts, then commit to that confidence. Since you know this solution works, don't try to fix it. It's a faith journey, but you are putting your faith in someone who has a guaranteed 100% success rate.

Chapter 9: Increase Beyond Measure

Now That's how I Want to Live My Life

One day, as I read the biography of George Mueller, a pioneer of faith and prayer, I came across a story that moved my heart. It was about a time when the orphanage Mueller ran had hundreds of orphans, but no money or food. In faith, Mueller asked the orphans to sit down at tables with empty plates in front of them, and said a prayer of thanksgiving for the food they were about to receive. When I read this, I thought to myself, "This is crazy faith! I would probably be freaking out and trying to find a way to get food before praying." George Mueller's faith challenged whether I really believed in a God who provides, is timely, and never fails us.

Mueller's story is about one of God's amazing provision miracles. As soon as they all said "amen," someone knocked on the door. It was a person with enough food to feed all the hungry children. What a wonderful testimony of how God provides for those in need in a timely manner.

As I read those pages, I was moved to tears and said in my heart, "God, I want to live my life this way. I want to have faith like George Mueller's and see Your miracles." This is a common response after reading or hearing testimonies of miracles and wonders. We want to experience them firsthand and personally witness God's power and glory up close. We know there is more to life than the monotonous treadmill of work or Sunday church duties. We know the miracle stories in the Bible and have heard testimonies from people who share about how God has done wonders in their lives.

For years, I longed to see the miraculous, desired to be a firsthand witness, and felt ready to be amazed by what God would do through our ministry. I believed that my intentions were noble, but my striving didn't lead to a dramatic shift in my experiences. I was confused because I thought my desires were in line with what God desired for my life.

I wanted to do great things for God, as many people do. Doing great things for God doesn't sound like a bad idea, until you realize that it makes you the protagonist of the story. *You* are the one doing great things. Self-promotion can be subtle, insidious, and deceptive. I was deceived into thinking that if I were to achieve great goals for God, God would get the glory through what I did for His Kingdom.

This realization deeply convicted me, and I decided to change my prayers to, "I want to do things for a great God." Moving the word "great" took the emphasis off of me, because the greatness I spoke of was only within God. Perhaps you, too, need a shift in your thoughts and prayers. It seems so subtle at first, but the results are astonishing. For me, one of the first results was God's miraculous provision at our aftercare home.

A Gift that Kept on Giving

After a couple years establishing our safe home for survivors of human trafficking, we were struggling as an organization to financially provide for all our beneficiaries' needs. We didn't have an annual budget that followed a strategic plan yet. We were just trying to serve to the best of our abilities, giving generously without considering our financial stability much. Our beneficiaries' well-being was our priority, and we had faith that somehow, God would cover all of our needs.

One day, a member of our church let us know about a man who was emptying a warehouse to make room for new shipments. He asked if we would be interested in receiving a donation of food, clothing, and other miscellaneous items. We said that we would be grateful for it.

The man had two employees fill up a moving truck with the donation, and they arrived at our safe house around five o'clock in the afternoon. I called volunteers to help unload the truck and about five young men showed up. We also contacted two other nonprofits who needed donations. Excited, they arrived shortly after the moving truck with vans to pick up some of the donation.

We filled two trucks and continued to take items into our safe house. We got food, office supplies, toiletry items, and an array of miscellaneous knickknacks. It was all stuff we needed. Most importantly, the donation included cookies, chocolate, candy, and chips, which were not a priority on our grocery list, but were definitely on our beneficiaries' list of desired foods.

Hours passed as we unloaded, and it started to get dark outside. The two warehouse employees were baffled. They couldn't understand why it was taking so long to unload the trucks, since it only took two hours to load them up. (Usually, it takes longer to load a truck than to unload it, as many of us have experienced when moving to a new house.) They also couldn't explain where all the stuff was coming from; it seemed to them that there was more coming out of the truck than they had put in. They kept unloading until close to midnight. Everyone was so busy trying to finish that we didn't take in the miracle that was happening before our eyes. A donation that took two hours to load took over six hours to unload. Even after filling two other vans, our safe house was so full of stuff that it was difficult to find space to walk in it.

A Shift in Mindset and Expectations

This experience of bountiful provision and miraculous multiplication made me completely rethink my personal expectations of what God can do. I found it interesting that we didn't lay our hands on the moving truck, asking God to multiply what we were about to receive. We also didn't make a supplication for provision before getting the phone call about a donation. God gave us what He knew we needed, and He even threw in some treats for our beneficiaries as a cherry on top of a beautiful ice cream sundae.

Reflecting on what happened, I was reminded of my prayer, when I said that I wanted to live my life like George Mueller, to have the same faith as he did, and to witness miraculous and bountiful provision. This was becoming my lifestyle now. Although it was never my preference to get to the point of not knowing how we'd see God provide, this experience increased my faith to know that all provision really does come from our Heavenly Father.

Still, when I didn't see a tangible way of meeting needs, I often stressed out, and anxiety dominated my thoughts. I frequently got busy contacting donors or publishing our needs online, soliciting monetary donations. I always thought I had to make things happen for our organization to move forward, and I believed deep down that my actions were more important than God's. I also thought that my concern and worries were being ignored, and my emotional engagement with our needs superseded my conviction to completely and totally depend on miraculous provision. I was starting to develop George Mueller's lifestyle of radical faith, but I was clearly uncomfortable and still stuck in my old mindset of working to deserve things.

Nevertheless, the first provision miracle we saw profoundly shaped my understanding of our divine relationship with our Heavenly Father. I began to see the special status that we all hold as daughters and sons of a loving and caring Father. Seeing myself as a beloved son was a paradigm shift from formerly seeing myself as a servant who arduously works in ministry. Divine provision embraces your divine identity. When I see myself and everyone we care for being loved by an outrageously generous Father, I am brought to my knees in humble and eternal gratitude. Allowing yourself this is an act of complete surrender, where striving ceases, and you fully let yourself be loved. You have to let go of all that you are holding on to, everything that brings you security, and allow yourself to fall into God's open arms. Surrender isn't always easy, but God's arms is definitely an easy place to be in.

The miracle also challenged my expectations regarding provision. To change them, it wasn't enough to move beyond my carnal efforts of fundraising towards surrendering my self-dependency. I had to alter what I expected God to do for me. I still believe that God answers our petitions and that He gives specific answers to specific prayers, but even my specific requests are limited to what I believe God can or intends to do for me.

Expectations often represent a limited view of the infinite blessings within God's storehouse. If I pray from a mindset with limited expectations, I make finite requests to an infinite God. If there are no limitations to my expectations, then anything is possible and my requests in prayer are presented in that mindset. It begins with our minds being transformed. First, we must let go of all of our presuppositions of what God can do for us. Then, we must know that all things are possible and all places are accessible. Knowing is not trying to convince yourself or thinking it's a possibility. Knowing is knowing.

In the Gospel narratives, Jesus refers to people's faith as "little" or "small." Jesus criticized what people believed was in God's range of possibilities. We all desire to have greater faith than the "little faith" Jesus referred to. The Bible tells us how our faith can grow. Romans chapter 10 talks about faith coming from "hearing the Good News about Christ." Hearing the Gospel creates faith, because the Gospel teaches us who Christ is and who we are in Christ. Faith is intrinsically tied to our identity in Christ, meaning our faith increases the more we understand our identity as God's children.

Just like our faith is intrinsically tied to our identity, our identity is also intrinsically tied to our community. Therefore, faith grows in the context of community. Our faith flourishes in the fertile soil of an encouraging and loving community. If we are isolated from community, when we go through personal struggles, our faith faces difficulties in growing and is sometimes stunted. That's why the enemy works hard to distance us from loving communities. We isolate ourselves for many reasons, including offense, lack of forgiveness, and disillusionment. To see our faith grow, we must not only grow in our understanding and practice being God's children, we must also stay connected to a Christ-centered community.

One of the key attributes of a Christ-centered community is compassion. Acts of mercy and compassion provide a near perfect atmosphere for signs, wonders, and miracles. Compassion provides a more ideal condition for the miraculous than any Christian conference or gathering on its own. We have countless testimonies of how God miraculously increased resources when we were serving others. There was a time that I believed abundant provision was only catalyzed by extreme need, but my personal experiences have since led me to believe that compassion is what actually provides the optimal context for abundant provision.

My petitions became less focused on what we needed as a family or ministry and more focused on how we could bless and serve others. I began to see how selfish it was to pray for increase when it was for personal gain or for our ministry, even if I knew we would be good stewards of our resources and bless others. What if I just prayed that others be blessed? God could then choose whomever He wants to bless. I examined myself and asked if my heart was truly genuine in its desire to see others blessed, or if my intentions were selfish—if I wanted to be the one used to bless. Rather than praying, "Use me, Lord, to bless others," I prayed, "Lord, bless those in need." Prayers like the latter one are true examples of hearts focused on God's compassion and blessings.

Abundance Comes through Generosity

Throughout history, Christians have frequently looked back on the first church community we read about in Acts chapter two, hoping to follow their lead. The first church is seen as a perfect example of a Christ-centered community. They continually met together to dedicate themselves to prayer and teaching disciples, shared their possessions, and served the needy in their community. God added to their numbers daily. Among everything that made this first faith community work, one key stands out to me most, which is that the first Christians were generous in heart and in deed. Generosity led to an abundance of grace and growth in their community. Generosity in heart was expressed through the absence of discrimination. The rich did not question why they had to share their possessions with the poor; there was no discrimination based on social class. Generosity in deed is observed in how no one in their community was in need. Imagine what it would look like if a church community today was so generous that there was no evidence of need among its members.

Abundance comes through generosity. Generosity unlocks Heaven's storehouse until our cups overflow. Many times, people wait for overflow before being generous, but we see in Scripture that God rewards those who cheerfully give, even when they are in need themselves. Being generous doesn't always have to mean giving a monetary gift. Just like the first Christians, we can be generous in heart and in deed. We can be generous with our time or with acts of kindness. We can also be generous in our grace and understanding of others. Even more challenging, we can be generous in our forgiveness of others.

If you have been contending to see more of God's miraculous provision in your life, remember to first seek the Provider and not the provision. Second, I encourage you to find ways to be generous towards others in heart and in deed. As you take generous steps, the focus turns away from your needs and towards the needs of others. Lastly, be proactive in your acts of mercy and compassion. The vast majority of Jesus' miracles happened when He was moved to compassion due to people's illnesses or states of need. As you reflect on God's merciful and compassionate heart towards others, your environment will be primed to see increase beyond measure.

Chapter 10: Restorative Healing

A Miraculous Restoration

One day, we received two young girls at our safe house who had been exploited by corrupt police officers. It was sad and infuriating to hear how they were abused and forced to prostitute themselves. The injustice made my blood boil. How could someone abuse their authority this way, banking on impunity because of their badge? This is one of many stories we come across in which the strong exploit the weak.

To add fuel to the fire, during the routine gynecological exams that all our beneficiaries go through, we learned that the damage to one of the young girls' reproductive organs was so severe that reconstructive surgery was recommended. When I heard this, the news hit me like a bombshell. What type of person would allow such destructive abuse to happen? Hearing stories of injustice like this over and over again can be infuriating, but I am convinced there is always also a God-story to be told, a story of redemption and restoration.

In addition to psychological therapies, our beneficiaries are always offered the opportunity to voluntarily participate in prophetic inner healing sessions with my wife, Janice. We see major breakthroughs from these sessions. People often receive healing from their deep past and present pain. Distraught from her diagnosis and the loss of her innocence, the young girl who needed reconstructive surgery participated in a session with Janice.

She was particularly troubled by the fact that she was no longer a virgin. Janice led her through a healing prayer and the young girl was able to envision herself pure and clothed in white. Visualizations such as this one remove the enemy's lies from us, allowing us to see ourselves just as God sees us.

A couple weeks later, at a follow-up consultation with the gynecologist, the doctor informed us that she no longer saw any evidence of physical damage to this young girl's organs. The doctor then said that in her professional opinion, according to the physical examination, the patient appeared to be a virgin. God not only healed this young girl, but also restored her completely. She no longer needed surgery. We were all amazed at God's miracle in her life. He took all of her mourning around her brokenness and turned it into joy!

Restoration and Purpose

Restoring a piece of art means reviving it to its former glory, so that people can admire the artist's original work. This process takes months or years of painstaking work and attention to all of the piece's intricate details. Still, this laborious work pales in comparison to the restorative work that God can and wants do in us. Just as God formed our bodies while we were in our mothers' wombs, He also had specific intentions and purposes for our lives since before we were born. I referenced this concept in an earlier chapter, calling it "original design." God's restorative work in us enables us to portray His glory the way He originally intended. Qualities and colors that are part of who we truly are may have been obscured by past pain. Just like the young girl from the story above, parts of us may have been damaged or stolen, keeping us from fully expressing who we were originally intended to be. God wants to restore us back to our original design.

As we are restored, our stories must be told. A restored masterpiece is not kept hidden in a closet but displayed in a museum to be seen and admired. Similarly, God's restorative work in us must serve a purpose. Part of it is to demonstrate God's power and glory to the world. Sharing your story is a powerful way to communicate how God both rescued and restored you. It may require a good amount of transparency to share painful parts of your story. Writing this book has been a way for me to share my story, and I hope that it encourages you to share yours, too.

Your testimony can encourage others. Every time I have the opportunity to share about how God transformed my pain into a platform for His glory, I encourage others. Sharing doesn't have to be dramatic, but it should be honest and heartfelt. When you share, you are never competing with others' stories, because yours is unique and special. Every story is an important contribution to the grand story of God's redemptive and restorative work on earth.

Pray for a Blessing

The end of Genesis 32 tells the story of Jacob wrestling with God. They wrestled throughout the night, and Jacob did not let go until he received a blessing. Jacob ended up receiving a new name, Israel, and being blessed by God. It's noteworthy that Jacob/Israel relentlessly contended with God until he received a blessing for himself.

It wasn't until learning that I could ask for a blessing for myself that I was truly able to understand God's heart. Before, I had believed that we could pray for others to be blessed, but that asking for a personal blessing was selfish or self-centered. However, I learned that the heart of God the Father is to richly bless His children. If the Father desires to bless His children, then it's logical to pray for a personal blessing.

Most of us feel more comfortable praying that God would bless others, since we know we should be generous and champion people's success. Asking for a personal blessing can feel awkward and too ambitious, but our Heavenly Father wants to lavish us with gifts and blessings.

> You parents—if your children ask for a loaf of bread, do you give them a stone instead? Or if they ask for a fish, do you give them a snake? Of course not! So if you sinful people know how to give good gifts to your children, how much more will your heavenly Father give good gifts to those who ask him (Matt. 7:9-11).

If you struggle asking for a blessing, remember who your Heavenly Father is. Consider James 4:2, which reads,

> You want what you don't have, so you scheme and kill to get it. You are jealous of what others have, but you can't get it, so you fight and wage war to take it away from them. Yet you don't have what you want because you don't ask God for it.

This is an open invitation to bring your requests before God, including asking to be blessed. I have often heard that we are blessed to be a blessing, and I believe it. However, we are also blessed to testify to the world that our God is the God of the universe, and He personally takes care of us. Knowing that I am blessed because I am God's child significantly changed my life and restored my heart by removing my orphan mentality.

When we understand that the context of a blessing is our sonship or daughtership, blessings take on a deeper meaning. Blessings are not just for our well-being and good fortune. They are a testimony of our divine adoption into God's family and they provide proof to the world that we receive Heaven's inheritance. For example, in the story of restorative healing at the beginning of this chapter, the young girl's vision of herself as pure and clothed in white was a reflection of how she is seen in Heaven. She was able to see herself as God sees her. The blessings, miracles, and healings that we experience here on earth are directly tied to our Heavenly identity.

There was a moment in our ministry when I knew we'd only get to our next stage of breakthrough if I fully manifested my spiritual heritage. On my father's side, there is a long lineage of pastors and missionaries. As a matter of fact, my ancestors were leaders in the first Christian church plant in their region of Korea after the arrival of the first missionaries. In other words, there is an apostolic spiritual heritage in my family line.

I approached my father, who also was a missionary in Latin America, and asked him to bless me. I knew I was already living out my spiritual heritage, but I also knew of the power of a blessing impartation from one generation to the next, a passing of the spiritual baton. Shortly after receiving a prayer of blessing from my father, we experienced enormous blessings and growth in our ministry. I knew I had access to all this, but it took a bold step of faith to ask for it. I learned that it's always in God's heart to bless us with His riches, the riches that affirm who we are as His children.

I encourage you to take time to find any gaps in your beliefs about blessings. Then, seek out blessings and become relentless like Jacob when he wrestled with God. Let that reform or remedy your view of our Heavenly Father. God is not stingy; He is generous and full of grace.

The Miracle in You is Greater

In our lives, all of us face mountains. In other words, we contend with overwhelming and insurmountable circumstances or challenges. Just remembering one of those moments can emotionally drain us. When we face mountains, we typically pray for the mountain to move. We reference Mark 11:22-23a, which reads:

> Then Jesus said to the disciples, "Have faith
> in God. I tell you the truth, you can say to this
> mountain, 'May you be lifted up and thrown
> into the sea,' and it will happen."

We pray for the mountain standing in our way to be removed from our path. We know it takes lots of faith, and it may take a miracle, but we feel like we need the mountain to move.   I love praying like this and seeing God move in miraculous ways, but through the years, I have also learned another prayer.

If we can also walk around or over the mountain, why do we prefer the mountain to move?   Are your current circumstances just an inconvenience or are they really keeping you from arriving at your destination?   Do you need the mountain to move because its ominous presence paralyzes you?   When walking around or over the mountain is not a viable option, and you haven't seen the breakthrough you expected, have you considered that it may be God's plan to make you bigger than the mountain, to the point that the mountain looks like a molehill to you?   There are times when the Lord wants to grow your character so that, when you face mountains, their sizes do not intimidate you.   Essentially, the miracle that God does *in* you is greater than the miracle He can do *for* you, and the miracle that God does *in* you is also greater than the miracle He can do *through* you.

Moving mountains might seem like an overwhelming task, and painful at times, but anything is possible with God. God's primary goal is not to remove obstacles from our paths. That would be convenient for us, but He has a greater purpose for the obstacles, which is the miracle He intends to do within us.   God's plan is to continue sanctifying us.   He focuses on what's inside. All external expressions of His glory and power must be rooted deeply in who we are in Him. God wants us to grow to be people with substance, not externally flashy people with empty souls.   As we look at the mountains in our lives, let's pray, "God, continue to do a miracle in me, so that I can overcome this situation."

Commit to growing into a spiritual giant who can step over mountains instead of remaining a spiritual infant.

In John 8:36, Jesus says that if the "Son sets you free, you are truly free." Through Jesus' victory of sin and death on the cross, we have been set free. If that's true, why do many of us still struggle with sin in our lives? Weren't we set free from it? In some ways, we may feel like we are still slaves to sin and not fully experiencing the freedom we have in Christ.

A prophetic friend of mine explained it this way, "For those who are in Christ, the opposite of slavery isn't freedom; the opposite of slavery is maturity." When I first heard that, it hit me like a ton of bricks. I cannot allow my experiences struggling with sin to negate the truth of my freedom in Christ. The truth of what Jesus declares over me, and the power of His resurrection within me, must supersede my experience. The issue becomes my level of spiritual maturity. If I am constantly battling against certain ungodly behaviors or attitudes, I am probably not mature enough in some area of my spiritual character that God wants to work on. Maturity does not come through simply trying harder. It comes from total surrender to the Lordship of Christ, complete dependence on the work of the Holy Spirit, and diligence with spiritual disciplines. Deliberate dedication to our spiritual development and formation is key to our maturity.

One practical step towards this end is to start applying this word to your life: congruency. Is your private life congruent with your public life? Are your thoughts and actions congruent with each other? Do your prayers asking

God for grace and mercy match the grace and mercy that you show others? Is how you love others in alignment with how God loves you? Be authentic and take off any facade. This develops integrity and character. This is how you will cultivate spiritual maturity in your life.

God deeply desires to do miracles in us, and He does that through developing our character and integrity. God wants all of us to grow up and become mature in our faith. At times, the process is going to be painful, but the experience will be invaluable. Miracles within us build maturity so that we can live in freedom and overcome any mountain we face on our path. This is what true freedom looks like.

About the Author

Benny likes to refer to himself as a "creative extremist," because today's social ills and injustices require creative means to bring about justice, reconciliation, and renewal. Benny and his team saw the injustice of global sex trafficking and decided to take action. They started rescuing, rehabilitating, and restoring trafficked victims in Mexico City and partnering with other organizations around the world.

The organization Benny and his wife Janice founded in Mexico, El Pozo de Vida, currently fights human trafficking through ten prevention, intervention, and restoration programs ("The Well of Life" - www.elpozodevida.org.mx). Benny also co-founded 27 Million (www.27million.com), a global network of grassroots organizations on the front lines addressing the issue of human trafficking. He has been identified as an Inspired Individual by Tearfund and holds an M.A. in Theology from Fuller Theological Seminary.

Benny is married to his lovely wife and they have two wonderful children, Charis and Micah. They have been living in Mexico City since 2007, where Benny and Janice are Senior Associate Pastors at Vereda Church (www.vereda.mx). Prior to this, Benny lived in the Washington metropolitan area, Asunción, Los Angeles, and Bangkok.

Made in the USA
Las Vegas, NV
09 May 2022